PUB W
NEA

Bournemo
Poo

G000152737

Other areas covered in the Pub Walks series include:

Bedfordshire
Berkshire
Birmingham & Coventry
Bristol & Bath
Buckinghamshire
Cambridgeshire
Cheshire
Chilterns
Cotswolds
Cotswold Way
County Durham
North & West Cumbria
South Cumbria
Dartmoor & South Devon
Derbyshire
Essex
West Essex
Exmoor & North Devon
Gloucestershire
Herefordshire
Hertfordshire
Icknield Way Path
Isle of Wight
Kent–The North Downs
East Kent
West Kent
Lancashire

Leicestershire & Rutland
Lincolnshire
North London
Middlesex & West London
Midshires Way
Norfolk
Northamptonshire
Nottinghamshire
Oxfordshire
Shropshire
South Downs
Staffordshire
Suffolk
Surrey
. Surrey Hills
Thames Valley
North Wales
South Wales
Warwickshire
Wayfarer's Walk
Wiltshire
Worcestershire
Wye Valley & Forest of Dean
East Yorkshire
North Yorkshire
South Yorkshire
West Yorkshire

A complete catalogue is available from the publisher at
3 Catherine Road, Newbury, Berkshire.

P U B W A L K S
——— N E A R ———
Bournemouth and Poole

Jack Street

COUNTRYSIDE BOOKS
NEWBURY, BERKSHIRE

COUNTRYSIDE BOOKS
3 Catherine Road
Newbury, Berkshire

ISBN 1 85306 403 3

Designed by Mon Mohan
Cover illustration by Colin Doggett
Photographs and maps by the author

Produced through MRM Associates Ltd., Reading
Typeset by Acorn Bookwork, Salisbury, Wiltshire
Printed by J W Arrowsmith Ltd., Bristol

Contents

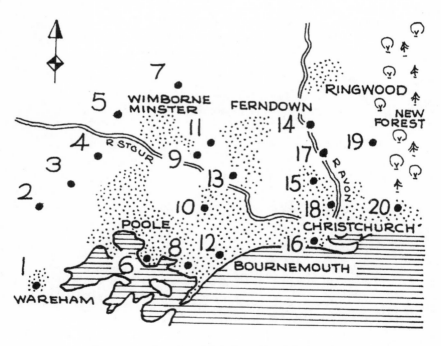

Area map showing the locations of the walks.

Introduction

Since Lewis Tregonwell, of Edmondsham House near Cranborne in Dorset, so liked the area now occupied by Bournemouth that he built the first house there in 1810, the town has grown to envelop the sandy ridges, valleys and heaths of its hinterland – part of Thomas Hardy's 'Egdon Heath'. Not only this, it has spread its suburbia in all directions to meet the houses of its historic neighbours, Poole and Christchurch, and almost Wimborne Minster. The latter has remained defiant, keeping the green ribbon of the lower Stour valley between it and the spread of red brick from the south.

There is a particularly fine coastline in these parts, with golden sands and soft sandstone cliffs, from Hengistbury Head in the east, an ancient monument dating back to the Stone Age, and around the curving sweep of Poole Bay to the Sandbanks peninsula. In the west of the area is Poole Harbour, the largest natural harbour in the world after Sydney in Australia. It has a shoreline of nearly 100 miles, enclosing about 10,000 acres of water. Once a thriving port, the old town of Wareham stands at the harbour's western end on the banks of the river Frome.

Inland, there are the wild acres of Canford Heath, culminating in a sandstone escarpment on its southern flank giving superb views over Poole and Purbeck. Further inland still are the green and pleasant valleys of the Stour, backed by the swelling hills of Dorset, and the Avon, flanked on the east by the sylvan beauty of Hampshire's New Forest. This area of contrast is finalised by the deep, silent ravines of the chines between Bournemouth and Poole.

All this makes a superb background for the 20 short and easy walks I have selected, and each characteristic of this varied landscape is encountered and savoured. The pubs are varied too, from the quaint old thatch of the Three Tuns at Bransgore and the ghostly flavour of the Old Thatch at Uddens Cross to the opulence of the Inn in the Park at Branksome Park. The area is full of interesting things to see and do, and an idea of other places that could be visited before or after the walk is given at the end of each chapter.

The sketch maps provided should be sufficient for route finding, but for added enjoyment you could also take an Ordnance Survey Pathfinder or an Outdoor Leisure map at the useful walking scale of 2½ inches to the mile, the relevant numbers of which are specified for each walk. Alternatively, you could choose sheet 195 in the Landranger series, which covers the whole area.

All start points for the walks are situated within ½ hour's drive of Bournemouth and Poole town centres in normal driving conditions. Many of the routes are truly rural, so be sure to wear suitable clothing and footwear. A walking stick is often handy in the countryside and binoculars, too, can be useful on occasions – but be careful not to clutter yourself. Finally, respect the Countryside Code by closing all gates behind you, remaining on the footpath, keeping dogs on a lead where there is livestock and leaving no litter.

Enjoy the walks and the pubs!

Jack Street
Spring 1996

Publisher's Note

We hope that you obtain considerable enjoyment from this book; great care has been taken in its preparation. However, changes of landlord and actual closures are sadly not uncommon. Likewise, although at the time of publication all routes followed public rights of way or permitted paths, diversion orders can be made and permissions withdrawn.

We cannot of course be held responsible for such diversion orders and any inaccuracies in the text which result from these or any other changes to the routes nor any damage which might result from walkers trespassing on private property. However, we are anxious that all details covering the walks and the pubs are kept up to date and would therefore welcome information from readers which would be relevant to future editions.

1 Wareham
The Quay Inn

The attractive Quay Inn has a broad, whitewashed frontage and paved forecourt and enjoys views over the old quay, the river Frome and the distant Purbeck Hills. You can sit outside this busy pub and imagine what the wharf was like centuries ago when ships carried merchandise to and from the port of Wareham. These were halcyon days before the Frome silted up and Poole took over as the main port in the area. Further misfortune occurred in 1762 when a pall of smoke hung over the town after the worst fire in its eventful history. Two cottages were built on the quay, as Wareham was gradually restored and over 100 years later one of these became a pub. Eventually, the other cottage was incorporated and the Quay Inn became as it is now – an unpretentious, cosy pub, with an arched brick fireplace and half-panelled walls.

Good ales are on offer here, including Old Speckled Hen, Boddingtons, Flowers Original, Whitbread Best and Pompey Royal, together with a guest ale (usually Ringwood Best). Heineken Export and Stella Artois are the lagers and a traditional cider is served from a barrel. Popular food choices are the pizzas, plaice and jumbo sausages, with home-made fisherman's pie a speciality. There is also a good selection of blackboard meals and a menu for children, who are welcome in the restaurant area. There is a small garden at the rear and picnic tables on the forecourt. Dogs are permitted outside, but not in the bar.

You can have a drink from 11 am to 3.30 pm and 6.30 pm to 11 pm on Monday to Saturday, and from 12 noon to 3 pm and 7 pm to 10.30 pm on Sunday. Food is available from 12 noon to 2.30 pm and 7 pm to 9 pm throughout the week. During the summer, when visitors flock to Wareham, the pub is open all day between Monday and Saturday.

Telephone: 01929 552735.

How to get there: Wareham can be reached by turning off the A351 Poole to Swanage road, which bypasses it. The pub is found on the left, at the lower end of South Street, just before you reach the bridge. The town has a station on the Poole–Dorchester line.

Parking: The inn has no car park but there is parking on the quay, with a maximum stay of 4 hours. Alternatively, there is a long stay car park at Streche Road off West Street. It is a 10 minute walk via Pound Lane to the quay.

Length of the walk: 3½ miles or 1½ miles if you choose the shorter Walls Walk route. OS maps: Outdoor Leisure 15 and Landranger 195 Bournemouth, Purbeck and surrounding area (inn GR 924871).

The Saxon earth walls, built to protect the town from marauding Danes, feature strongly in this walk. They are well preserved and signed. The shorter route makes a complete circuit of the ramparts, while the longer one takes you out beyond the walls to return by way of Wareham's interesting main street.

The Walk

Turn left from the inn and left again up an alleyway to emerge into Church Green. Walk over to the parish church of Lady St Mary, where Christians have worshipped for 1,300 years. The church was closely linked with the priory, now a hotel to the right.

From the church, go left along Church Street as far as The Cottage, where you turn right along Church Lane, noting one of the many signs sited to keep you on the route of the Walls Walk. The lane turns left, then right through the large churchyard to another left turn. Where the lane veers left, go straight ahead up a grassy bank to join the first part of the ancient walls. Continue along the crest, dipping briefly to cross over Bestwall Road. Young elms now line the route until the ramparts swing left around the perimeter of an open space known as the Bowling Green,

where fairs were once held. There are good views to your right over the river Piddle to Northport and the distant conifers of Wareham Forest.

Descend to Folly Lane, going right, then left into St Martin's Lane. Just past St Martin's Close, turn right to join an oak-shaded path called Ladies Walk. Pass the ancient Saxon church of St Martin and turn left to North Street. Cross over North Street, turning right down the hill to Shatters Hill on the left. Walk up the hill to rejoin the walls by taking the metalled path up the bank on your right. There are fine views again to your right as you arrive at the north-west corner of the ramparts, called the Cockpit. Where paths cross, turn right down into the trees, taking the right-hand path up to Streche Road as the ways divide.

For the short route, keep straight ahead up the bank at the path crossing, then down Pound Lane and back to the quay.

For the longer route, continue along Streche Road, with the hospital to your right, turning right as you reach the entrance to Lady St Mary School. A gravel track takes you downhill, under the bypass and then sharp left to the gate leading into West Mills. Pass to the left of the gate and turn right to pass the mill, built around 1700. Cross the river Piddle and follow the track as it bends left to go under the railway. Take a green track, slightly right-handed, towards a distant gate, with a ditch on your left. Go around the gate to follow a track on the right. This leads over flat, marshy land which forms a part of the river Piddle's floodplain. Soon the green track turns left to cross two ditches before dwindling to a path and bending right behind the rear fences of houses. Pass through a kissing-gate in the corner to join a confined path.

Cross over a road to follow the path as far as the next road, where you turn right. This is Careys Road, which takes you past shops to eventually meet Bere Road. Go right to cross the railway line at ground level (there is also a footbridge), just to the north-east of Wareham Station. Proceed on the road past the Railway Tavern, until you see a motor sales area to your left. At this point, take the metalled pathway branching right, leading to a subway under the bypass. Continue to the road and cross North Bridge over the river. Go straight ahead, up the hill and walk down North Street to The Cross, and then along South Street, back to the Quay Inn.

Places of interest nearby

Wareham is an interesting old town and well worth a stroll round to see the fine buildings and churches. Look in at the town museum in East Street near The Cross and visit the information bureau nearby. You could also discover Dorset's first toy and musical box museum at *Arne* (cross South Bridge and take the first left). On the A351 towards Poole, you may care to pull into the *Sandford Pottery* to see local products – this area is rich in high quality clay.

② East Morden
The Cock and Bottle

You will discover the fine Cock and Bottle in a pleasant valley, with gentle green hills swelling up all around. This is a good example of a Dorset long house, in which the dwelling area and stables are behind one continuous façade. Morden is a charming, scattered place linked by narrow, winding lanes and dominated by the Victorian church on the hill. It is a secluded village and well worth a visit.

The Cock and Bottle, which had a thatched roof until as recently as 1966, is a welcoming pub, popular with locals and visitors alike. The old long house now forms a series of bars adjacent to the road and is the most ancient part of the inn, at least 300 to 400 years old, and the original ceiling and an exposed bit of cob wall can be seen in this section. The rear of the building is of a later date and leads out to a pleasant little patio with tables. The intriguing name is, we are told, shared with only four other pubs in the country.

This is a Badger house and you can sample Badger Best, Tanglefoot, Hard Tackle and Charles Wells Eagle. For cider lovers there is keg Dry Blackthorn and a good range of lagers and wines is also available. There is a comprehensive regular menu, listing, for example, venison poivrade, lambs' kidneys sauté and various fish dishes, followed by an interesting choice of desserts. This is supplemented by appetising blackboard specials such as pigeon breast and fresh local plaice. Children are welcome and have their own menu. Well-behaved dogs are allowed in the pub, too.

The inn opens its doors from 11 am to 2.30 pm and 6 pm to 11 pm on Monday to Friday. The hours are the same on Saturday, but with a longer lunchtime, to 3 pm. Sunday opening is from 12 noon to 3 pm and 7 pm to 10.30 pm. Food is available from 12 noon to 2 pm every day and from 6 pm (7 pm on Sunday) to 9 pm.

Telephone: 01929 459238.

How to get there: Morden lies about 1 mile north of the A35 Poole to Dorchester road. Leave the main road at Park Corner and take the B3075, northbound. The inn is on the left after ½ mile.

Parking: There is ample parking to the side of the inn.

Length of the walk: 4 miles. OS maps: Pathfinder 1319 and Landranger 195 Bournemouth, Purbeck and surrounding area (inn GR 912946).

An attractive mix of country lanes and field paths awaits you as you walk around the pleasing village of Morden. There are splendid pastoral views made possible by a softly undulating countryside.

The Walk

Leave the pub and cross the road to enter one of the many picturesque lanes which serve this spread-out community. There is a telephone kiosk and a postbox on the corner. Proceed along the lane to pass Sticklands House Farm and take the next turning left. Walk up to a left-hand corner and go right through Sellers Farm. Keep to the right of a brick barn to cross the stile (or go through the adjacent gate). Head across to the far left-hand corner of the meadow, where a stile is visible to the left of a cottage. Cross this and keep to the right-hand edge of the next field. A little way along, the path turns right to a narrow 'squeeze' stile at the end of a row of concrete garages. Go through the stile and turn left to pass by the front of the garages. Follow the access road, which veers left into a short cul-de-sac of houses. Turn right and then left as you meet a lane.

Walk up the sunken lane to Morden's triangular village green, where you keep to the left-hand side. The dominating church is to the right if you wish to visit it. The Erle Drax family, who lived at nearby Charborough House, are much in evidence inside the church and there is an impressive monument to Thomas Erle who died in 1597. Cross the road and take a track to the right of a bungalow, The Glebe. Veer slightly left

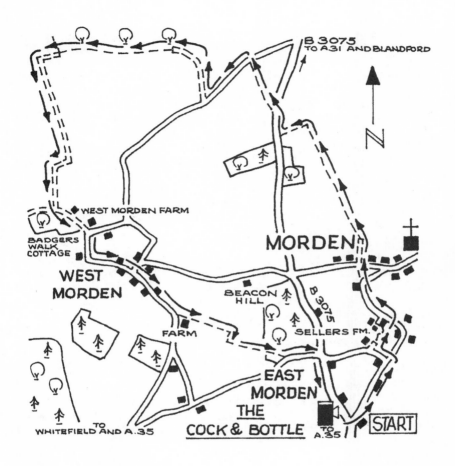

at a gate to see the path rising up to a metal gate some distance ahead. Pass through this and enjoy the view over the Winterborne Valley, with Charborough Tower showing over to the right. This was erected in 1796 and is 120 ft high. It was not greeted with enthusiasm when it was built, but provided the inspiration for Thomas Hardy's novel *Two on a Tower*.

I found the best route from here was to the right of the hedge, where the farmer had left a clear strip between the hedge and a cereal crop (even though the OS Pathfinder shows the path to be to the left of the hedge). At the bottom of the field, turn left and walk along to a gate. Pass through and turn right onto the road. As this soon bends slightly right, look for a stile in the left-hand hedge – there was no step when I passed and it is easy to miss it. Cross the stile and go half-right across the field to the visible stile opposite. Here you meet a lane and turn left. Soon you turn right onto a trackway, which you follow to shortly swing left. This continues as a path along the left-hand edge of a field to soon become tree lined. Go through a metal gate to be joined by a path from the right.

The path becomes a track again, swings left and climbs up through peaceful countryside to a wooded knoll, where you join another track. Go left here and descend to the hamlet of West Morden. As you meet a lane by West Morden Farm, keep straight ahead to bend left by Badgers Walk Cottage. Proceed by pretty cottages, past where a lane joins from the left, to cross a waymarked stile on the left as the lane bends right at a farm. Keep ahead along the right-hand margin of a field, with the farmhouse on the right, and maintain your direction down into a small valley. Soon you reach a fence with an unused stile to the left. Pass through a gap in the fence and bear right to a field corner, where you go left at right angles and walk up the right-hand side of a field to reach a stile. A woodland path now takes you ahead to reach a lane after crossing another stile. Turn left on to the lane as far as the crossroads, where you go right and walk past the village shop and post office to return to the pub.

Places of interest nearby

Not too far away, if you return to the A35 at Park Corner, turn right and then take first left towards Bovington Camp and Wool, to find Lawrence of Arabia's home at *Clouds Hill* (telephone: 01985 847777) and the *Bovington Tank Museum* (telephone: 01929 463953 (answerphone) or 405096). There is also *Monkey World* at Longthorns close by, where primates can be seen in a natural environment (telephone: 01929 462537).

Lytchett Matravers
The Chequers Inn

3

This is a fine 17th-century pub and it was here that tenant farmers on the vast Drax estate used to come regularly to pay their rents. Charborough House, set in many acres of ground to the north, was the impressive home of the family. Lytchett Matravers has a traditional and rather sinister ring to it, and it was Baron John Maltravers (the letter 'l' has since disappeared from the village name) who was involved in the murder of the wretched Edward II at Berkeley Castle in 1327.

The Chequers, with its cosy, intricate bar and attractive restaurant, looks onto the High Street at the west end of the village, which is, like the inn, a mix of old and new. Enter the pub and you will find some interesting little plaques set upon the beams in the bar. One refers to Samuel Crumpler who was a maker of coffins in 1801. This is a true Dorset surname, and wherever in the world you meet a Crumpler you can be sure that the family tree will be traced back to the county. These days many of the villagers work in nearby Poole and its surrounding area.

Good food is readily available at the pub and is listed on a fancily presented bar menu, with a separate one for the restaurant. The choice is extensive and includes a range of steaks, pies, grills, basket meals and fish dishes. Vegetarians are well catered for and children can tuck into their own favourites, such as Golden Tiddlers and Lamb Boomerangs. This is a John Devenish house, but you can also enjoy guest ales like Bass and Worthington. Strongbow cider is available and the pub specialises in country wines. There is a good sized garden at the rear with amusements for children. Well-behaved dogs are allowed in the bar.

The Chequers opens its doors from 11.30 am to 2.30 pm and 6 pm to 11 pm on Monday to Friday. The hours are the same on Saturday, except that lunchtime is extended to 3 pm. The Sunday times are from 12 noon to 3 pm and 7 pm to 10.30 pm. Food is served from 12 noon to 2 pm every day (with a limited lunch menu in the restaurant on Wednesday and Thursday) and, in the evening, from 6 pm to 10 pm on Monday to Saturday and 7 pm to 9 pm on Sunday.

Telephone: 01202 622215.

How to get there: Lytchett Matravers lies to the west of the A350 Poole to Blandford road. Leave the main road at Jubilee Cross (Barrow Hill) and proceed into the village, turning right into the High Street. The inn is on the left.

Parking: There is ample parking at the side of the inn.

Length of the walk: 2 miles. OS maps: Pathfinder 1319 and Landranger 195 Bournemouth, Purbeck and surrounding area (inn GR 941955).

You will enjoy the fine rolling countryside on this walk, passing by the lovely old church of St Mary the Virgin in the valley, peaceful and serene in its woodland setting. As with many remote churches, it is normally kept locked, but names of keyholders are displayed. In springtime the woods are a colourful haze of bluebells, and throughout the year there are pleasant views over the fields to the high woods of Charborough Park.

The Walk

Leave the Chequers and turn left along the High Street. Continue past the Jenny's Lane turning and then look out for a large house on the left, named Lytchett St Mary, which used to be the rectory. Immediately after this, turn left through a metal pedestrian gate onto a tree-shaded path. Bluebells abound to your right in springtime, while open country unfolds to the left as you gradually descend to where the path bends right.

Ignore the stile on the left and continue down to a pedestrian gate leading into Lytchett Matravers churchyard, which you enter. Walk around the church's short, stocky tower to emerge via a gate into the car park beyond.

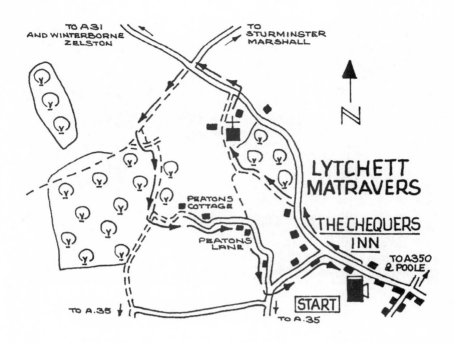

The tower is the oldest part of this fine stone church, which dates back to Norman times. It was the centre of the village in those days, but the ravages of the 14th-century Black Death caused the dwellings to be moved up the hill to healthier parts. There are six bells in the tower, three of which were there in the reign of Edward VI (1547–1553).

Walk down the lane to join a road. Turn left and continue for nearly ¼ mile to where Dullar Lane enters from the right. Opposite, up a bank to your left, you will find a stile. Cross this and follow a defined path along the right-hand edge of a field. Cross two more stiles near a metal gate. A further two stiles bring you into woodland. It could be muddy here so watch out. Where the path soon forks, bear right up a shallow bank and look for a left-turning path at the top. Follow this to join a track and go left. As the track swings left, you arrive at a metal gate. Go up to the gate and turn right to follow a path alongside a wire fence. This path is an escape route if the main path on your right is muddy. You will find many of these escape paths to avoid possible muddy parts as you go ahead along the inner fringe of woodland.

Cross a stile and then turn left to join another path. If this is muddy,

Lytchett Matravers church.

there is an alternative route on the left which avoids the worst. The path bends left and then takes up the mantle of a track. This track is short lived as it soon becomes a metalled lane, passing Peatons Cottage on the left.

Follow the attractive, winding Peatons Lane uphill past a mix of modern and older housing until you reach Jenny's Lane. Turn left into Jenny's Lane to continue your toil uphill past the wrought iron gates of Chartley to the junction with the High Street. Turn right and make your way back to the Chequers.

Places of interest nearby

Some 5 miles to the east are the twin attractions of *Merley House* and *Merley Bird Gardens*. The house itself is an exhibition centre, as well as being an 18th-century showpiece with fine Georgian plaster ceilings. It is open from 10.30 am to 4.30 pm daily between Easter and October (telephone: 01202 886533). Just over the road are the bird gardens, with formal and water gardens as well as exotic birds (telephone: 01202 883790).

Corfe Mullen
The Coventry Arms

④

If you have never seen a 500 year old cat, come to the Coventry Arms! This moggie is in a mummified state in a glass case and the poor thing was found in the attic during alterations several years ago. Hundreds of years past, a dead cat was considered useful to ward off evil spirits. The Coventry Arms dates back to 1426, only eleven years after Agincourt. It later served as a coaching inn and, together with nearby St Hubert's church, a manor and several cottages, made up the village of Corfe Mullen. The plague dealt harshly with the settlement and, in common with many other similar villages, it was moved from its riverside spot to supposedly healthier ground higher up – where the modern, developed, Corfe Mullen is now. The church, pub, manor house and cottages, however, stayed where they were.

Don't let the mummified cat spoil your appetite, as the pub food is excellent. There is a good, varied menu and tempting specials on the board, like grilled whole Poole Bay plaice, chargrilled Wensley pork chop and spinach tortellini filled with ricotta cheese. The bar menu offers a range of starters, salads, ploughman's lunches, main courses, chargrills, vegetarian dishes and filled baguettes. There are also various fillings for jacket potatoes, children's meals, puddings and a Sunday roast with all the trimmings. Food can be ordered at the separate food counter adjacent to the restaurant area, but you can eat anywhere in the pub or outside on the patio. The Coventry Arms is noted for its real ales including Old Thumper, Ringwood Fortyniner and Bass, and weekly changing guests, such as Flowers Original and Abbot Ale, all straight from the barrel. Alternatively, what about Newquay Steam Bitter, or Newquay Steam Pils, Heineken and Stella Artois lagers, or draught cider and stout? This ancient pub with its flagstone floors, double fireplace, five interconnecting bars, low doorways and antique furniture is well worth a visit and well-behaved dogs on a lead are welcome.

The opening hours are from 11 am to 2.30 pm and 5.30 pm to 11 pm on Monday to Saturday, and from 12 noon to 3 pm and 7 pm to 10.30 pm on Sunday. Food is available every day from 12 noon to 2 pm. In the evening it can be ordered from 6.30 pm to 9 pm on Monday, 6.30 pm to 9.30 pm on Tuesday to Saturday, and 7 pm to 9 pm on Sunday.

Telephone: 01258 857284.

How to get there: The Coventry Arms lies 2½ miles west of Wimborne Minster on the A31 Dorchester Road.

Parking: There is parking to the rear and the side of the pub.

Length of the walk: 2½ miles. OS maps: Pathfinder 1319 and Landranger 195 Bournemouth, Purbeck and surrounding area (inn GR 973985).

Wooded knolls and hills separated by green valleys are a feature of this circuit, together with lanes framed by high hedgerows. It is a quiet, pleasant part of Dorset, on the western fringe of the Poole conurbation. There is a lovely old church at the end of the walk, beautifully maintained and worth exploring.

The Walk

Step outside the Coventry Arms and cross the A31, with care, to join Brickyard Lane opposite. You soon pass over the old Somerset–Dorset railway line, opened in September 1862 and affectionately known as the 'Slow and Dirty'. Another lane joins yours from the left, but keep straight on ahead, noting the metal gates leading to a landfill area on the left. This was the site of old clay workings, which explains why Brickyard Lane is so called. There are other active workings away up to the right. Veer left along a track and look out for a stile on the left by a metal gate. Cross the

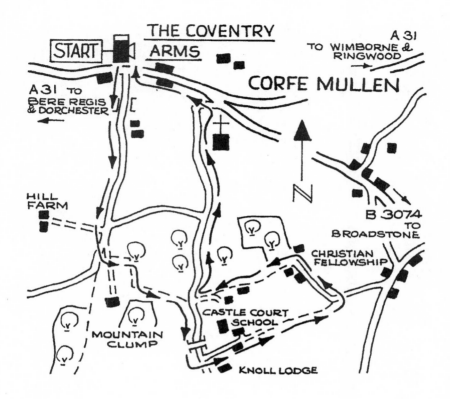

stile and follow the left-hand side of a meadow uphill, with a barbed wire fence to the left. Climb up to a large oak tree at the bottom of a steeper bank. Turn right here and follow the base of this bank past a gnarled oak. Gradually curve left up the bank towards a stile visible in the fence ahead, to the left of woodland called Mountain Clump. Pause on your way to admire the fine view over the valley and woodland to the right.

Pass through, or over, the stepless, waymarked stile and head to the right of a white-rendered house in the valley below. Descend the meadow to a stile you will find to the left of a corrugated barn and a clump of ash trees. Cross the stile to join a lane and turn right. Follow this shaded, winding lane uphill past a school sign and then downhill under a metal bridge, which connects the school to its playing fields. The Castle Court Preparatory School was formerly called Knoll House and was occupied by one John Coventry in the mid-19th century, the estate covering a large area. The pub you have just left had several names over the centuries, including the Cock and Wheatsheaf and the White Lion. When John Coventry acquired the land, the inn was then renamed in his honour.

Turn left off the lane into the school entrance and walk up past Knoll Lodge, with the school buildings on the left. The metalled road soon becomes gravelled and finally dwindles to a fenced path leading down into a valley. Go past a horse stable to meet an access drive. Turn left uphill towards what used to be Knoll Farm and walk forward past white-washed cottages on the left to enter the pea-shingle of the old farmyard. The farm became a Christian Fellowship Centre in 1984 and now offers smart convention facilities. Turn left and head for a wide, grassy, fenced path indicated by a waymarked post. Follow the footpath as it descends gently and curves right, then left past a well-positioned house with fine views over the Stour valley. Cross the stile to join an access track leading straight ahead to meet a lane you will recognise.

Bear right and walk down the lane for a good ½ mile until you reach the main road. If you have time, go right and visit the parish church of Corfe Mullen, dedicated to St Hubert. This is a picturesque old church and was, until 1858, a chapel attached to nearby Sturminster Marshall. It is very ancient, with the east window of the chancel being some 700 and the nave 500 years old. From the bottom of the lane you left to visit the church, turn left to walk the short distance along the main road and back to the pub.

Places of interest nearby

Corfe Mullen is only 2½ miles from *Wimborne Minster*, where there is much to see. Look around the Minster itself, with its famous chained library, visit the craft centre at Walford Mill and enjoy the model town and gardens, and the Priest's House Museum. Telephone the information centre on 01202 886116 for further details.

Pamphill
5
The Vine Inn

If you want to visit a pub with the smallest bars you have ever seen, come to the Vine Inn, deep in a National Trust landscape at the fascinating village of Pamphill. Time has really stood still at this village inn, which began life as a bakehouse and later became a cider and alehouse. The proverbial cat could only be swung round with difficulty downstairs, but the hospitality is first class. The premises have been in the same hands for three generations already and look like continuing in the same way.

In the homely bars, Whitbread Best and Strong Country Bitter are on offer, together with Heineken lager, a guest ale and Bulmer's or Inch's draught cider. There are also country wines like cherry, apricot and damson. Emphasis here is on the drinks, but from 12 noon to 2 pm each day you will find a good range of sandwiches (toasted or plain) and ploughman's lunches. If the weather is fine, there is plenty of room in the front garden where about 20 tables are laid out in pleasant surroundings overlooking the valley. Even though the two bars are tiny, well-behaved dogs are allowed in them. For families, there is a room upstairs which can be used if necessary.

On Monday to Saturday the inn is open from 11 am to 2.30 pm (3 pm

on Monday) and 7 pm to 11 pm. On Sunday the times are 12 noon to 3 pm and 7 pm to 10.30 pm. There is no food in the evenings.
Telephone: 01202 882259.

How to get there: Pamphill lies about 1 mile to the west of Wimborne Minster. Take the B3082 out of the town towards Blandford Forum. Turn left shortly after passing the school and leisure centre on the left into a lane signed to Pamphill. Turn left again and then take the left-hand fork. The pub is on the left.

Parking: There are a few spaces on the lane outside. If these are full, there are public car parks up the lane near the cricket pitch, about ten minutes' walk away.

Length of the walk: 3 miles. OS maps: Pathfinder 1300 and Landranger 195 Bournemouth, Purbeck and surrounding area (inn GR 994003).

This walk offers a fine variety of true Dorset countryside, with shady lanes and a picturesque church in a lovely pastoral setting. The whole village of Pamphill and the surrounding area was bequeathed to the National Trust in 1981 by Ralph Bankes of Kingston Lacy House. There has been no development in the village and it retains a stately feel of rural splendour.

The Walk

From the Vine Inn turn right to walk up the lane past a cream-washed cottage to a triple-armed footpath sign which announces the Stour Valley Way. Turn right as far as an electricity pylon and then go right-handed over a stile and down into a valley, where you will find a four-armed sign-post. Turn left to cross a footbridge and a stile. A sign indicates that this is a conservation area. With a stream on your right, follow the path up a valley and over another stile. Cross a footbridge and walk up through bushes and scrub to cross over a stile on your right, as another path joins from the left.

You now cross a footbridge and, as the path forks, go left uphill on a well-defined route through woodland. This is all a part of the National Trust owned Kingston Lacy estate, with paths, signs, stiles and waymarking maintained by the Trust. Your path curves down to the right over board-walks to a stile. Ignore the path to the right and cross over the stile. You now enter a sloping meadow, where you walk half-right down to a stile and a footpath sign. Cross the stile and head for the left-hand side of a timber-framed, thatched cottage. Look out for a stile to your right to cross and enter the garden of the cottage. Do not worry about this as it is a

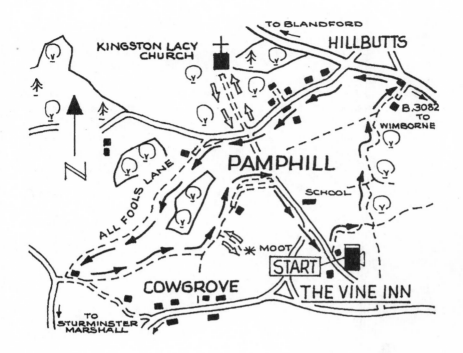

public right of way. Go left-handed onto a shingle driveway which you follow to join the main Wimborne to Blandford road. Turn left and walk along the narrow pavement with care. It very soon widens and you arrive at a crossroads, where you turn left to go along a lane past Hillbutts post office and the village hall. You may wish to drop in at the Pamphill Dairy Farm Shop a little further along for a look around and a coffee.

Soon you arrive at the lovely approach drive to St Stephen's, Kingston Lacy, on the right. It is well worth strolling up to this fine church, admiring the manicured grass verge on the way. Look out for the beautiful copper beeches and a newly planted red oak tree. The church is open on Saturday and Sunday afternoons (2 pm to 5.30 pm) and also on bank holidays from Easter to the last weekend in October. It is not an old church, being built in 1906–7 by Henrietta Bankes of Kingston Lacy House in memory of her husband.

Return to the lane and resume the direction you were following, looking out for a well-trodden diverging path on the left. Join this and soon turn left onto an access track. As this bends right to a cottage, go ahead on a hedged pathway. This is All Fools Lane, a delightful, shady

27

path which you follow downhill past two pairs of gates until you reach a track with cottages on the left. Turn left past the front of these and look for a stile on the left adjacent to a metal gate. Cross this and take the direction of the waymark arrow obliquely right over arable land to another stile. Go over this and maintain your line of direction over a field to a visible stile. You will find this an interesting path as you cross this stile and another to the right of a rusty gate. Note the direction of the waymark arrow over each stile – this is especially important when the next stile is not in view. After you have crossed the stile by the rusty gate, your path goes over a hill, down to encounter two more stiles and up over another hill to a stile in the hedge, followed by a footbridge.

Here you join another path and turn left, crossing a further stile to go up the right-hand side of a meadow. Negotiate another stile and turn left. If you have 15 minutes to spare, go right here and visit 'The Moot'. You will find an information plaque on the far side of a mounded area. Returning to the route, proceed along an enclosed path through a gate to join a track. As this bends right, go ahead into the playing field area, turning right to pass the thatched pavilion to join the lane. Turn right past the school, built in 1698, keeping ahead at the road fork, back to the Vine.

Places of interest nearby

Pamphill adjoins *Kingston Lacy Park* with its stately home owned by the National Trust. It is a 17th-century house built for Ralph Bankes' ancestor and namesake, Sir Ralph Bankes, and contains a fine set of paintings. There are 250 acres of parkland all open to the public. For details of opening times, telephone: 01202 883402.

Poole
The Portsmouth Hoy

6

On the quieter, western side of Poole Quay, away from the ice-cream and pleasure boats, you will find a quaint little old inn looking more like a cottage than a pub, but with its name written proudly and large on its frontage. Step inside this spotless place of gleaming brass, with its lovely blue, sea-like carpet, furnished with well-polished tables and smart uphol-stered, round-backed chairs, and soak in the nautical relics and equip-ment all around you, from carpet to walls and up to the flag-painted ceiling – a virtual maritime museum. But why Portsmouth Hoy? And what is the name of a rival south coast port doing on the sanctum of Poole Quay? A hoy is a small 18th-century vessel or barge which carried cargo and passengers over a short distance, so the Portsmouth Hoy was prob-ably such a craft, trading regularly between Portsmouth and Poole. There has been a building on this site since 1736, although the original would have been a wooden structure.

The menu lists the tenants of this Eldridge Pope house since 1879, as well as announcing some mouth-watering dishes, with a natural inclination towards fish. The 'Fishy Affairs' section offers Old Smokie (haddock with a cheese sauce), battered calamari and grilled whole fresh plaice. There are also many dishes for meat lovers and vegetarians, in addition to burgers, ploughman's lunches, jacket potatoes and sandwiches. A specials board changes daily and, next to this, you will see a children's menu and desserts. The selection of ales is wide, with the full range of Eldridge Pope beers on tap, like Best Bitter, Indian Summer, Hardy County and Royal Oak. Lager comes in the form of Carlsberg, Carlsberg Export and Kronenbourg, and draught Dry Blackthorn cider and Guinness are available. There are wines to suit all tastes, too. This pub is popular and becomes very busy in summer. There is no garden but you can sit out on the small forecourt and watch the world go by. Dogs are not welcome in the pub, except for guide dogs.

Quench your thirst here between 11 am and 11 pm on Monday to Saturday, and between 12 noon and 10.30 pm on Sunday. Food is available from 12 noon to 9.30 pm every day.

Telephone: 01202 673517.

How to get there: The pub lies towards the western end of Poole Quay, west of the ferry and pleasure boat terminals.

Parking: The pub has no parking facilities, but you can park on the quay itself (max 4 hours), or in the multi-storey car park off West Street.

Length of the walk: 3½ miles. OS maps: Pathfinder 1301 and Landranger 195 Bournemouth, Purbeck and surrounding area (inn GR 007903).

The north shore of Poole Harbour gives superb views over the water to Brownsea Island and the other islands, with the hills of Purbeck as a fine backdrop. The walk takes you along to enjoy these views and then turns inland to the attractive Poole Park and its lakes before returning to the quay.

The Walk

Begin by turning left from the pub, crossing the road and walking on the seaward side of the quay, past the pleasure boat moorings, each displaying their own tour guide map of the harbour. Continue to the lifeboat station, where you veer inland to pass around the building, opened in 1882. This is usually open and admission is free. The earlier station was at North Haven Point on the Sandbanks peninsula. Briefly join Ballard Road to go round a left-hand bend, turning immediately right to walk along a walled, concrete path. Go over a slipway, with the Fisherman's Harbour, protected by a breakwater, to the right, to join a metalled path beyond.

Follow this water's edge pathway and enjoy the views across the

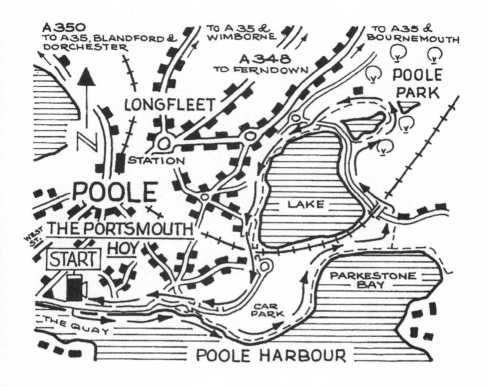

harbour. Go past Baiter car park and then around the head of Parkstone Bay to cross the sluice controlling water from Poole Park lake. About 200 yards further on, look out for a gravel path to the left. Ahead of you is an opulent white-balconied house with a prominent white-stepped wall fronting it. Walk up to the wooden fence and turn left, either over the low stile, or through the gate, to join Whitecliff Road and proceed ahead to the railway arch. Pass under this with due care (fortunately the traffic is light) and emerge to view the fine, extensive lake to the left. There is a model yacht enclosure on the nearside. Walk along the lakeside road to pass the five columns of the old park gates, the side pillars mounted with eagles and the centre three supporting short lamp standards.

Go past a road hump and turn right onto a metalled pathway, with the Poole Park model railway on your left. Walk over a 'level crossing' as the path bends left and the railway passes over to your right. There are glimpses of a smaller lake through trees to the left which is heavily populated with swans, Canada geese, mallards and an assortment of domestic ducks and sea birds. Just along the path, you encounter a railway junction, with a branch line forking right to nearby engine sheds. Follow the path around to the left to share a bridge over a water channel connecting two smaller lakes where swans will gather, expecting food, if you pause there. Go past the Poole Park station, with a building housing a children's adventure playground and an adjacent café on your right. You finally say goodbye to the model railway as it loops left and you cross over a park road towards the big lake and a small car park.

Turn right to pass through the car park and take the lakeside path ahead. Pass under an oak and walk through neat, hedged war memorial gardens back to the lakeside. Go to the right of a tree-shaded enclosure and proceed straight ahead past a children's play area on a mound to the right. As you meet Park Lake Road, veer left to the lakeside again to soon fork right, passing under the Bournemouth – Poole railway to join Catalina Drive. Walk ahead, with new housing to your right. Soon the road bends right, and if the day is clear, you may see Corfe Castle perched on its conical mound in a gap in the Purbeck Hills over 6 miles away as the crow flies. Pass Labrador Drive to reach the junction with Furnell Road on the right. Turn left here and cross the road to the left of a semi-detached house. Rejoin the harbourside path right-handed, back to the pub.

Places of interest nearby

At Poole, there are many attractions to look around, such as the famous *Pottery* (telephone: 01202 666200), the *Aquarium* complex (telephone: 01202 686712) and the *Waterfront Museum* (telephone: 01202 683138). All of these are to be found on the quay. Additionally, why not enjoy a road train ride for ½ hour around the town – you can join it on the quay. There are also pleasure boats if you fancy a cruise.

7 Holt
The Old Inn

Village inns and parish churches quite often cohabit very well and, in so doing, set up an aura of peace and contentment. So it is with the Old Inn, St James' church and rural Holt. When you visit, you may have the impression that the inn doesn't quite look like a pub – a more apt description would be a Victorian wide-fronted house with a good covering of Virginia creeper. This feeling is promptly dispelled, however, as you enter via the porch (look out for the old pump and letterbox) and you are greeted by a pleasant bar, a red carpet, timber-framed walls with brick nogging infills and wood-burning fireplaces at each end. This is a fine, out-of-the-way, early 19th-century hostelry.

A Hilaire Belloc snippet on a beam in the bar observes: 'When you have lost your inns, drown your empty selves – for you will have lost the last of England'. This, fortunately, is not the case yet. A Badger house, the Old Inn offers BXB Bitter, Badger Best and Tanglefoot, with Pilsner and Hofbrau lagers. The food menu is extensive, giving a wide selection of good, well-presented dishes, ranging from prime fillet steak and mixed grill to trout almondine and breaded plaice. There are home-made pies, basket meals, salads, ploughman's lunches and assorted sandwiches, as well as a specials board. Vegetarian tastes are well catered for, too. Children are permitted in the no smoking family area and there is a large rear garden for sitting out in fine weather. Dogs are welcome here, but not inside the pub.

The inn is open from 11.30 am to 3 pm and 6 pm to 11 pm on Monday to Saturday, and from 12 noon to 3 pm and 7 pm to 10.30 pm on Sunday. Food is served from 12 noon to 2.30 pm every day and, in the evening, from 6.30 pm to 9.30 pm on Monday to Friday, 6.30 pm to 10 pm on Saturday and 7 pm to 10 pm on Sunday.

Telephone: 01202 883029.

How to get there: Holt is just over 2 miles north of Wimborne Minster. Take the B3078 out of the town and, after 1 mile, you will see a turning signed to Holt on the right. The Old Inn is on your right in the village.

Parking: The pub has several parking spaces on its frontage and there is a large overflow park across the road.

Length of the walk: 3 miles. OS maps: Pathfinder 1301 and Landranger 195 Bournemouth, Purbeck and surrounding area (inn GR 030039).

Much of this area is dairy farmland on the western edge of extensive heathland. Initially the walk takes you over lush meadowland before it enters the southern fringe of Holt Forest, which is an ancient woodland of oak, beech and holly.

The Walk

From the Old Inn turn left and walk alongside the church wall. The church was built in 1834–5 on the site of a former chapel and the wall was added a year later. Where the road forks, turn left, pausing to admire the view on your right over the green to cottages on the Wimborne road. Look for a stile on your left before you reach a bungalow on the same side. Cross the stile and, keeping the hedge on your left, cross two more stiles before a third leads you out onto a farm track by a large oak tree.

Follow the track straight ahead until it bends sharply left. At this point, keep straight on into a meadow and head for a stile visible in the right-hand hedgerow, just beyond the first oak tree. Pass over the stile and walk obliquely left across another meadow to a metal gate in the far left-hand corner. Go through this to cross the stile immediately on the right. Again head obliquely left across another field, keeping to the left of a lone midfield oak tree. You will find a further stile in the hedge a little forward of the left-hand field corner, where your path is joined by another from the right. Cross the stile and then, keeping the hedge on your left, go

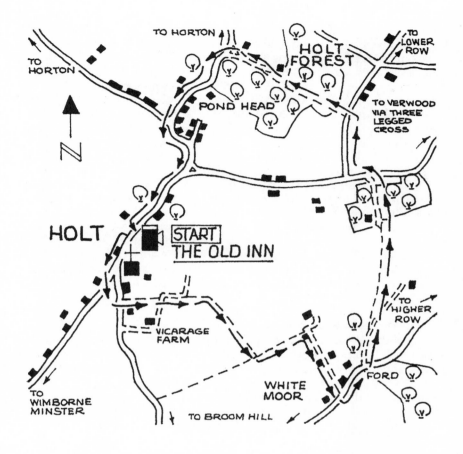

over two more stiles to emerge onto an access track known as Sheepcroft Lane, where you turn right.

The lane soon becomes metalled as you pass through the hamlet of White Moor. Look out for the attractive Willow Cottage on the left before you arrive at a lane. Turn left to follow the lane past Whitemoor House to arrive at a ford. Veer left and cross the stream by a footbridge. This stream is one of the feeders to Uddens Water, which joins the Moors river near Trickett's Cross, some 2 miles away. After going over the footbridge, look for a track and a blue bridleway arrow on your left. Join this to follow a pleasant trackway to where a path angles left just before the track rises up a slight incline. Take the path, which soon narrows to enter woodland and then leads uphill to eventually join a track. Follow this past buildings on the left to meet a road. About ½ mile to your right lie the 1,200 acres of Holt Heath, which is one of the largest remaining heathlands in Dorset and became a National Nature Reserve in 1985.

As you meet the road, turn left and then immediately right up a lane signed to Lower Row. Walk along it until it swings slightly right after crossing a little bridge with white side fences. Look for a bridleway sign with a blue arrow on the left. Another sign announces that you are entering Holt Forest, which is another National Nature Reserve and contains some fine oaks. It was referred to in the Domesday Book as part of the Forest of Wimborne. Take the left fork inside the wood to follow a path which is often muddy – this is a poorly drained area. Soon you emerge from the trees to pass to the left of a bungalow and shortly meet the access road to it. Walk left-handed away from the bungalow, with the nursery grounds of Glen Farm on the right. Soon you reach a road after passing a display cabinet, which usually contains self-serve fruit and vegetables.

Turn left and follow the road (Pond Head) down into a valley and then steeply up again past houses to the junction with Lodge Road. Turn left and walk along this road, past a junction and then uphill, back to the Old Inn.

Places of interest nearby

A trip to the *Dorset Heavy Horse Centre* can easily be made from Holt. It lies about 1 mile to the north of Verwood at Brambles Farm, Edmondsham. There are some fine Shire horses here in stables or in harness, with examples of horse-drawn farm machinery (telephone: 01202 824040). A mile away in the village is *Edmondsham House* and gardens, which are open to the public at times. This was the home of Lewis Tregonwell, who built the first house in Bournemouth in the year 1810 (telephone: 01725 517207).

8 Lilliput
The Beehive

At the same time as disillusioned and brave folk were setting out from these shores to a new, free life over the Atlantic in 1620, a building was erected in Lilliput which is now the Beehive. Today, the establishment is large and caters well for the neighbourhood and passing trade, but you can still see relics of the old pub, which used to be a coaching inn on the sandy road between Poole and Christchurch, long before Bournemouth was ever thought of. The name is probably derived from The Hive, a nearby aristocratic clergyman's residence, and in the spacious bar, you will see many local monochrome photographs of the area as it used to be.

Until fairly recent times, the Beehive was a hotel in this favoured holiday and leisure locality. Now owned by Eldridge Pope, it serves as a popular and thriving pub. It is a relaxing, roomy place with a long, angled bar and subdued lighting. Step inside and enjoy ales such as EP Best, Dorchester, Royal Oak, Hardy Country and Indian Summer, with Tetley Bitter as a back-up. There is a good selection of lagers, including Castlemaine XXXX, Carlsberg Export and Kronenbourg. Guinness and Dry Blackthorn cider are also available on tap. The restaurant area to the rear of the pub overlooks a wide lawn backed by trees. A varied menu offers food from Hardy's Kitchen, with appetisers like Japanese prawns and chicken satay and a good range of main courses – for example, mushroom stroganoff, vegetable tikka masala, rack of lamb or a 12 oz rump steak. Daily specials appear on a board, together with a choice of desserts. You can also eat in the bar or out in the garden. Children are welcome and dogs are permitted in the garden but not inside the pub.

The pub is open from 11 am to 11 pm on Monday to Saturday, and from 12 noon to 3 pm and 7 pm to 10.30 pm on Sunday. Food is available from 12 noon to 2 pm every day and, in the evening, from 6 pm to 9.30 pm on Monday to Saturday and 7 pm to 9 pm on Sunday.

Telephone: 01202 708641.

How to get there: The pub lies near to the shops in the centre of Lilliput, on the B3369 road between Poole and Sandbanks.

Parking: There is ample parking on the left-hand side of the pub.

Length of the walk: 2 miles. OS maps: Pathfinders 1301 and 1334 and Landranger 195 Bournemouth, Purbeck and surrounding area (inn GR 038900).

There is a surprising number of woodland footpaths in suburban, well-heeled Lilliput. The walk includes a large and attractive sample of these before emerging onto the fine Poole Harbour shoreline, then to enjoy glorious views from the romantic Evening Hill, from where sunsets over the water are really superb.

The Walk

From the pub frontage cross the main road with care and turn left, then quickly right to join Blake Dene Road. Walk up this leafy road to arrive at an open space on the right opposite Austin Avenue. A footpath sign points right and indicates 'Footpath 57 to Brownsea View Avenue'. Follow this pathway, with trees and bushes closing in before you emerge onto the road. Cross obliquely right to where Footpath 57 is signed through to Anthonys Avenue. The path is confined between a lap larch fence and trimmed close-set trees. Go over the road to resume your progress along Footpath 57. These suburban footpaths have been carefully preserved from the days when this area was rural, and they are very well signposted. As a wire mesh fence on the left angles sharply left, you will find that the path divides. Turn left and take the shady path with school grounds and distant buildings on the right. This path soon turns right to lead down between fences, past the Lilliput First School buildings as far as Lilliput

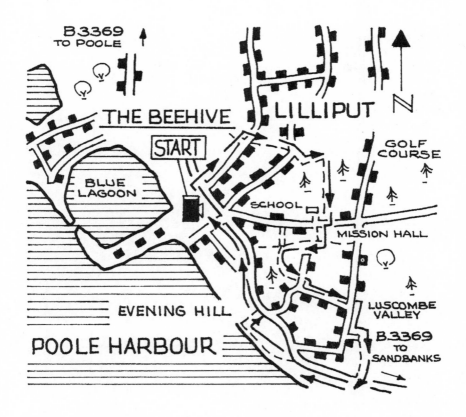

Road opposite the picturesque Lilliput Mission Hall.

Cross the road with care to go obliquely right to join Footpath 71, signed to Crichel Mount Road and Avalon. Walk up this confined path until you reach a junction of paths, where you go right. This is a pleasant, shaded path which curves gently to emerge soon at the top of Lilliput Close. Turn left to join the unmetalled footpath leading uphill through holly bushes (do not take the metalled path further to the right). It is difficult to believe that you are in the midst of residential development as you begin to descend and then rise steeply through woodland to meet Crichel Mount Road. Go half-right to join Minterne Road, which you follow downhill, turning right at the bottom into Alington Road. Cross over to the other side and take the second turning left into Alington Close. Walk the short way down this cul-de-sac to join the signed Footpath 85 right-handed down to Shore Road.

A fine view opens up before you over the waters of Poole Harbour,

39

Evening Hill – panoramic views of Poole Harbour.

with the Sandbanks peninsula and the long, wooded line of Brownsea Island quite prominent. Brownsea Island is owned by the National Trust and is the home of red squirrels and the many peacocks and peahens which strut around imperiously. Lord Baden Powell held his first camp for 20 Boy Scouts here in 1907. To the left, on the north side of Shore Road is the Luscombe Valley Nature Reserve. Cross the road and turn right. To the left, you are almost sure to see windsurfers enjoying their sport in the shallow bay. Walk along the recently improved promenade up to the East Dorset Sailing Club, which celebrated its centenary in 1975 and is the oldest club in the harbour. Just after passing the club, turn left down steps to enter the car park, where you turn right to pass onto a metalled waterside path. You will not be able to keep your eyes away from the fine views of the harbour, with the romantic backcloth of the Purbeck Hills beyond. It is amazing to learn that its shores stretch for nearly 100 miles and that it is second in extent only to Sydney Harbour.

Soon the path ends and you climb the steps to the top of Evening Hill. Pause here awhile and take a seat to enjoy the panoramic views. When you have had your fill, turn left on Sandbanks Road and stroll downhill past Dorset Lake Avenue and the shops of Lilliput, back to the Beehive.

Places of interest nearby

If you care to drive out to *Lytchett Minster* just west of Poole, you will find the Courtyard Centre in Huntick Road which houses country arts and crafts, a pets' corner and gardens, together with Dylans Restaurant (telephone: 01202 623423). *Upton House* and its country park are also close by, between Poole and Lytchett Minster, and are worth a visit (telephone: 01202 672628). *Brownsea Island* is open to the public from Easter to early October, 10 am to 8 pm (or dusk, if earlier). There is a regular ferry service from Poole Quay every half hour (telephone Poole harbour: 01202 707744). There is a restaurant and shop as you disembark from the ferry. As the island is owned by the National Trust there is a landing fee for non-members but a reduced rate is available for families and parties.

Little Canford
The Fox and Hounds

9

How pleasant it is to find a quiet backwater like Little Canford, where modern development has bypassed this corner of old Dorset in the lower Stour valley. Roads which used to be through routes are now country lanes. Houses once shaken by passing traffic are now havens of peace. The river Stour wanders down from the weir near the famous old Canford School, through lush pastures and past sleepy lanes on its way to Christchurch Harbour.

The attractive Fox and Hounds, with its thatch and open surroundings, is situated at the end of a short driveway. This fine inn dates from the 18th century, the oldest part being on the right by the bar area. Here you walk on venerable flagstones under very low beams. Just beyond, there is an alcove which is dedicated to Canford School and its history.

The pub is a Wayside Inn and offers a choice of eight real ales, four of which, Pedigree, Boddingtons, Wadworth 6X and Flowers Original, are regular. The other four change at intervals. There are Heineken and Stella Artois lagers and Strongbow cider, supplemented by a good selection of wines. The range of food is wide and varied, and you can choose from the bar menu or from the specials board, and children have their own bill of fare. Main courses include a vegetarian selection, together with pies, steaks and chops, sometimes a mega mixed grill. Fish is also prominent and there is usually a traditional fish and chips meal. A good selection of desserts is available to follow. There are wide, open lawns to the side and rear where you can sit with your food and drink on warm days. Amusements are available for children and dogs are permitted in that part of the bar which has a stone floor.

This is a twelve-hour pub, so you can enjoy a drink between 11 am and 11 pm on Monday to Saturday, and from 12 noon to 10.30 pm on Sunday. Food is available between 12 noon and 10 pm (9.30 pm on Sunday). Telephone: 01202 872881.

How to get there: Turn off the B3073 Christchurch to Wimborne Minster road just south of the A31 roundabout at the eastern end of the Wimborne bypass. The inn is down Fox Lane and to the left.

Parking: There is plenty of parking at the front of the pub.

Length of the walk: 3½ or 4½ miles. OS maps: Pathfinder 1301 and Landranger 195 Bournemouth, Purbeck and surrounding area (inn GR 045000).

This is an enjoyable walk, which begins on the banks of the river Stour amid lush green meadowland, and you will see the fine old buildings of Canford School coming ever nearer. Then you cross flat meadows, with a glimpse of the distant towers of Wimborne Minster, before you head back to the inn. You have the option of adding a waymarked stroll through the woodland of Leigh Common.

The Walk

Leave the pub and walk down to the lane, where you turn left. As you meet another lane opposite to Manor Farm, turn right. At this junction, look for the signpost which indicates Castleman's Trail, the route you are following. Castleman was the designer of the Southampton–Dorchester railway via Ringwood. The line had so many twists and turns that it was called Castleman's Corkscrew and Dorset County Council are trying to use the old railway track as a path, but not all sections have been acquired from landowners at present.

Follow the lane almost to the A31. Cross the stile on your left to head slightly right-handed over a meadow on this well-used section of Castleman's Trail. Two more stiles follow before the path angles further right, with a glimpse of the river Stour nearby on your left. You are now heading for the distant buildings of Canford School and soon the path

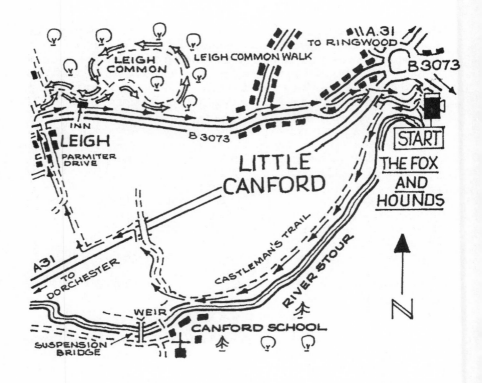

takes an attractive route along the river bank. A line of willows along a depression to the right marks an old watercourse. Admire the stately architecture of Canford School on the far bank. This has been a school since 1923 and has had a good academic record over the ensuing years as well as a fine sporting tradition.

The path now veers away from the river as a weir comes into sight, and heads towards a gate with a stile on the right. Cross this and reluctantly part company with Castleman's Trail and its green train logo as it turns left. Your route is right-handed along a track which crosses the Wimborne bypass by a high bridge. From this point, the towers of Wimborne Minster are clearly visible to the left. Cross a stile to the left to descend steps and follow a fenced path alongside the A31. Cross another stile and go right-handed over a field, heading for a gap in the far left-hand corner, where you meet a track. Turn right and soon join Parmiter Drive, a pleasant road of bungalows. Follow this to emerge onto Leigh Road.

You now have two options. If you decide to include the Leigh Common circular route, which adds 1 mile to the walk, cross over Leigh Road to

Canford School, seen across the Stour.

join Northleigh Lane. Immediately turn right onto a gravel road called Leigh Common. Just before semi-detached houses on the left, turn right by a sign announcing the common. Follow the path into woodland and take an interesting round trip indicated by green arrows.

From the junction of Parmiter Drive and Leigh Road, turn right (or left if you have favoured the Leigh Common option) and pass the Sir Winston Churchill pub, to continue along the wide, grassy verges of Leigh Road. Shortly after passing Sydney Winchcombe Tom's seat (installed by his family for his 80th birthday), cross over the road. Note the fine bungalows and manicured gardens of The Acorns as you head eastwards. Just before you reach the Murco Garage, turn right to follow a lane under the bypass and back to the pub.

Places of interest nearby

The *Avon Valley Country Park*, just off the Three Legged Cross to Ringwood road, is well worth a visit. It has much to amuse children, including a fine model railway which you can ride on. There is also a pleasant lake and an excellent adventure trail which involves a 'tree tops' walk. You can get there by driving along the A31 towards Ringwood and turning left onto the B3072 to Three Legged Cross. Turn right and after nearly 2 miles look out for the signs.

West Howe
The Shoulder of Mutton

Time has passed by this attractive old village pub. A spread of modern housing and commercial development has generally crept upwards and outwards from Bournemouth and Poole to smother village centres and cottages – but not so the Shoulder of Mutton, which stands bypassed on a lane, remaining happily unchanged. It is the third oldest hostelry in Bournemouth and began its life as a pub in 1851. Before that, it was a baker's and a butcher's, which explains its name. Augustus John often visited this inn to meet the characters he used in his paintings. There is a ghost here too and it has made its presence felt on many occasions. You are unlikely to see it, however, in pub opening times.

This is a Whitbread house and provides the usual range of their beers. Ales like Ringwood Best and Fortyniner and Flowers Original are also on offer. Lager lovers can enjoy Stella Artois, Heineken and Heineken Export, and there are a couple of wines on tap, together with Guinness and cider. The two bars (Village and Lounge) give the pub a cosy atmosphere and you can eat in either. A simple printed menu includes homely food, such as cottage pie and sausage with chips, but you will also find dishes like chicken Madras or lamb balti. A specials board offers, for example, sea food platter or a selection of home-made pasties. The lounge bar has small, friendly tables and green-upholstered, wheel-backed chairs, with some interesting old local photographs on one wall. Outside, there are picnic tables on the forecourt and a grassed area to the left of the pub, with more tables and some children's amusements. Dogs are not allowed.

The pub is open from 12 noon to 3 pm and 6 pm to 11 pm on Monday to Friday, 12 noon to 4.30 pm and 7 pm to 11 pm on Saturday, and 12 noon to 3 pm and 7 pm to 10.30 pm on Sunday. Food is served at lunchtime between 12 noon and 2 pm (2.30 pm on Saturday) and can be available 'by arrangement' in the evening.

Telephone: 01202 573344.

How to get there: The A348 (Ringwood Road) between Poole and Ferndown passes through West Howe. Proceeding northwards on the A348 from the Wallisdown Road roundabout (where the A3049 from Bournemouth joins the A348) to the next roundabout, take the parallel service road to the left immediately after the roundabout. The pub is further down on the left, past the post office.

Parking: There is ample parking to the left of the pub.

Length of the walk: 3½ miles. OS maps: Pathfinder 1301 and Landranger 195 Bournemouth, Purbeck and surrounding area (inn GR 053958).

The enclave in the Poole residential area provided by the wild, remote acres of Canford Heath is prominent in this walk, which is firstly and lastly suburban but, in between, sandy paths take you up to the crest of the heath to enjoy views over the bustle of Poole, its famous harbour and the distant hills of Purbeck.

The Walk

Leave the pub and turn left along the service road, which was the former lane leading down to rural Bear Cross. You may have noticed an old photograph in the pub's lounge bar which showed Bear Cross as it was at the turn of the century. Walk along past attic windowed bungalows and turn left past three concrete bollards into the cul-de-sac known as Deepdene Lane. This soon joins Knighton Heath Road, but before the actual junction, turn right onto a metalled footpath, crossing over to join High Howe Lane on the left. Go up the hill and fork right into Spicer Lane, where pleasant houses lie behind oaks on the left. Walk forward past the Weldon Avenue junction to enter the Borough of Poole. Where the road ends, go forward on a wide metalled footpath past concrete bollards and

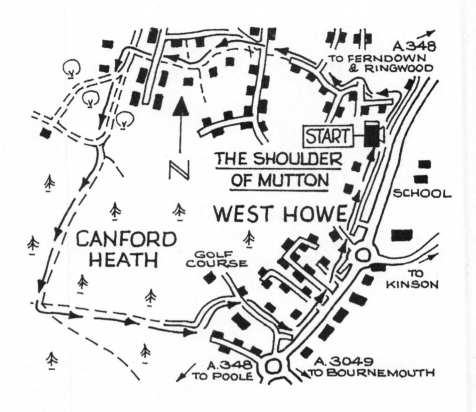

down sharply, crossing Knighton Road to continue ahead on another footpath. Follow this as it curves left, passing four bollards and going uphill, with trees to the right and a wooden fence to the left. This is a semi-urban pathway known as Wheelers Lane – a relic from the rural past.

The pathway descends to a staggered crossing of paths, where you go directly ahead uphill to cross over Viscount Walk. You now join a continuation path, which is gravelled and quickly leads you to a leafy, narrow metalled lane. Turn left and walk up a gentle hill to a parting of ways, where you go left-handed along a track behind houses. This becomes lined with gorse bushes and takes on a sandy texture as you leave the houses behind. Trees close in before the track bends to the right (ignore another path going left here). Walk up a gentle slope, with a barbed wire fence on the left and firstly woodland, followed by open heathland, to the right. Heather, gorse and bracken dominate as the path steepens and then

The path across Canford Heath.

levels out, with a high, pine-dotted ridge on the skyline ahead. As the ridge draws closer, the path inevitably steepens to become rutted with gouged out water channels. Eventually, your toil brings you out to the ridge top path, where you turn left.

From the ridge there is a view over Poole and its harbour to the hilly spine of the Isle of Purbeck, which, on a clear day, is worth at least a few moments' pause to take it all in. Follow the ridge path eastwards as it passes through dwarf gorse before becoming a metalled track and turning sharp left as you approach a substantial concrete fence. Continue ahead and soon go round a right-hand bend by a tall, steel communications tower. Pass to the right of a road grid via a metal kissing-gate to join the access road to Northbourne Golf Club. Turn right here and walk down Francis Avenue, with bungalows to the left and the premises of Bournemouth and West Hampshire Water to the right. Go ahead past a junction and join Ringwood Road past black and white bollards.

At the main road, turn left past the pelican crossing, walk for ½ mile to approach a roundabout and join a service road fronting shops. Cross over High Howe Lane and proceed across the frontage of the Clock Garage to walk down the service road, past West Howe post office and back to the pub.

Places of interest nearby

The *Tower Park*, situated along the road towards Poole, is described as 'so much fun, it shouldn't be allowed'. There is a ten screen cinema complex, eight water slides and rides, thirty computerised bowling lanes and an ice rink, not to mention cafés, restaurants and bars. Telephone: 01202 715040 (cinema), 716123 (water rides) and 716000 (ice rink).

⑪ Stapehill
The Old Thatch

If you are looking for a ghost, come along to the Old Thatch at Uddens Cross and savour the possibilities! If you ask the manager nicely, he will drag out a sheaf of press cuttings telling you all about the ghost which has caused one predecessor to flee in terror and another to fall down the stairs. The problem was so acute at one time that Whitbread appointed two managers, neither of whom were to stay in the building at night. This long, low, thatched building was once the entrance lodge to the nearby Uddens house. When this was consumed by fire many years ago, a heavily carved mahogany door was retrieved from the ruin and installed at the inn – and it can be seen today, looking decidedly sinister and almost evil, just inside one of the entrances. There is an opinion that this ornate door may be at the root of the problem. Even now, there are strange happenings and sensations.

Coming back to reality, the inn has a picturesque appearance with its thatch and latticed windows. Inside, there is a good, spacious bar and a restaurant. The area on the right is the oldest part of the pub, built in 1742, and the low oak beams are genuine. Not so the left-hand side, which was added later and fashioned to look like a part of the original.

There are special menus, one for bar food and the other for the restaurant. The bar menu offers a choice of omelettes, curry and rice, steak and kidney pie, gammon with egg and pineapple, plaice and chicken tikka, or ploughman's lunches and sandwiches. The restaurant à la carte menu lists 15 main dishes and a good selection of desserts. In addition to Whitbread ales, you can sample Flowers, Boddingtons and Wadworth bitters. Strongbow cider is available on draught and there are a number of wines. Children are welcome. Dogs are not allowed in the restaurant area, but a bowl of water is provided for them in the main bar! There is seating outside for when the weather permits.

The inn is open from 11 am to 11 pm on Monday to Saturday, and from 12 noon to 10.30 pm on Sunday. Food can be ordered from 12 noon to 2.30 pm (2 pm on Sunday) and 6 pm (7 pm on Sunday) to 9.30 pm. Only the bar menu is available on Sunday evening and on Monday.

Telephone: 01202 877192.

How to get there: The inn is situated at Uddens Cross to the east of the Stapehill roundabout on the old Wimborne to Ferndown road, which can be reached from the A31.

Parking: There is ample parking at the rear of the pub.

Length of the walk: 2½ miles. OS maps: Pathfinder 1301 and Land-ranger 195 Bournemouth, Purbeck and surrounding area (inn GR 053005).

Much of this walk takes you through woodland and over typical Dorset heathland where pine, birch, gorse and heather are dominant. There is a section of road walking, but there is a pavement and a verge.

The Walk

Leave the pub and go left into Uddens Drive to cross over Wimborne Road, which was the former A31. Proceed along Stapehill Road to pass the exit from Stapehill Abbey. This was a Cistercian abbey, an order which originated from Citeaux in Normandy. Houses soon appear on the left and, at this point, take a track to the right and walk past the Forestry Commission sign reading 'Stapehill'. Beech and oak shade this pleasant trackway, giving way to pines before you reach houses. Where the track divides opposite Sansoms Cottages, go left to eventually pass Marchant's Wholesale Nursery and soon reach Stapehill Road again.

Cross over to take the right-hand track. Ignore a left-branching track named Award Road. Continue through pines and rhododendrons to pass

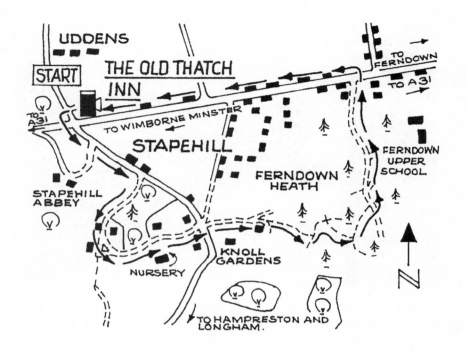

a cottage on the right. Go forward, ignoring a track marked 'private' on the left. Where your track turns right, go ahead on a footpath to pass, via a walk-through stile, onto heathland. This is a wild area of pine, gorse and heather. Ignore all side paths as your route gradually swings in a general left-hand direction. When you arrive at a junction, go left onto a wider path, which soon bends right. As you meet a cross path, turn right and head towards a metal gate with a stile on the left.

This area is characteristic of the Dorset heathland that dominates the south-eastern part of the county. Some 3,000 years ago, in the Bronze Age, the existing forests were cleared by man for use as farmland. The exposure resulted in leaching, and the loss of nutrients in the acid soils meant the land became too poor to support crops. This led to the heathlands we see today. There is evidence of controlled burning to restrain the spread of gorse.

Cross the stile and turn left, with the fence on your left, until you meet a sandy track where you turn left. Follow this well-used path, keeping straight ahead over a cross track. Electricity transmission lines close in from the left and you soon pass under them. They continue to keep you

A lonely track on Ferndown Heath.

company for some distance on your right-hand side. Away to the right over a shallow heathland valley you will see the modern buildings of Ferndown Upper School. Watch out for wildlife on the heath, including the sand lizard and smooth snake. Adders like to bask in the sun on warm days, so look out for them.

At a path junction, veer left to remain on the principal path. Keep an eye open for the preying hobby, which is a small, long-winged falcon, and the stonechat (a little thrush-type bird with black and white markings). Woodlarks and the Dartford warbler also inhabit these heathlands. Very soon, you leave Ferndown Heath to meet Wimborne Road, where you turn left. Follow the road for a little over ½ mile back to the inn. There is a pavement all the way with grassy verges over most of the distance.

Places of interest nearby

Just along the road is the entrance to *Stapehill Abbey* and its fine grounds. The gardens, with their rock pools and waterfalls, have won awards. There is a working craft studio to visit and an original farmhouse. You can obtain refreshments at the coffee shop and browse in the gift shop. The opening times are 10 am to 5 pm, every day from Easter to 31 October, closed on Monday and Tuesday between 1 November and Easter (telephone: 01202 873060).

12 Branksome Park
The Inn in the Park

Deep in the leafy opulence and wealth of Branksome Park, this fine looking, bay-windowed, red-brick inn fits its surroundings well. It is a popular pub, standing off the beaten track and much frequented by local people. Subdued music of a lightly classical nature greets you as you enter its roomy, sectioned bar, tastefully decorated, with the large bay windows giving plenty of light. There is a small paved area with tables and chairs, outside at the front. This is much in demand when the sun shines warmly, as it often does in these favoured parts.

The comfortable and hospitable Inn in the Park offers you a choice of Wadworth 6X and Henry's IPA, Bass and John Smith's Bitter. Those who prefer lager can enjoy Carlsberg or Stella Artois, and there is draught cider and Guinness, backed by a good selection of wines. You can sit down to good food either in the bar or in the restaurant. The lunchtime menu includes beefburgers, curries and pastas, in addition to a vegetarian choice like vegetarian stroganoff or quiche. A 'chef's special' board tempts you with dishes like lamb chump chops, chicken breast in red wine and poached plaice roll. There is also a good menu for children as well as salads, ploughman's lunches, freshly cut sandwiches and desserts. The evening menu offers an even wider choice. Well-behaved children are welcome in the pub. Dogs are not permitted in the restaurant, but may come into the bar area.

The opening hours are from 11 am to 2.30 pm and 5 pm to 11 pm on Monday to Friday, from 11 am to 3 pm and 6 pm to 11 pm on Saturday, and from 12 noon to 3 pm and 7 pm to 10.30 pm on Sunday. Food is served from 12 noon to 2 pm and 6.30 pm to 9.30 pm each day, but the restaurant is closed on Sunday and Monday evening.

Telephone: 01202 761318.

How to get there: From the County Gates Gyratory, take the B3065, to go down The Avenue signed to Sandbanks, past the Western Road traffic lights, to turn left into Tower Road. The inn is just over ½ mile on the right along this road and into Pinewood Road.

Parking: The inn has a moderately sized car park, but you can park in Pinewood Road or down in the Branksome Dene Chine car park.

Length of the walk: 3½ miles. OS maps: Pathfinder 1301 and Land-ranger 195 Bournemouth, Purbeck and surrounding area (inn GR 066901).

The famous deep, wooded chines just to the west of Bournemouth are the background to this walk and three of them are visited. These are Branksome, Branksome Dene and Alum Chines. In addition to the quietness and wooded splendour of the ravines, the walk includes a bracing stroll along the promenade.

The Walk

Step out of the inn to turn left along Pinewood Road and quickly go right to join the access road down to the Branksome Dene Chine car park. Pause to have a look at the mausoleum on the left and to read the information plaque behind the railings. The Packe family home at Branksome Towers became a very high class hotel, often visited by royalty, approached by a fine driveway, now named The Avenue. The old hotel was demolished in 1973 and replaced by flats. At the far end of a wooden-boarded fence to the right, you will see a footpath sign showing a route to the beach. Follow this path, ignoring steps down to the left, and descend steeply to the promenade below, where you turn right. Old Harry Rocks and the long, curving line of Ballard Down are straight across Poole Bay. To the left, you can see Hengistbury Head, the Needles and, on a clear day, St Catherine's Point, the most southerly point of the Isle of Wight.

A sylvan path in Branksome Chine.

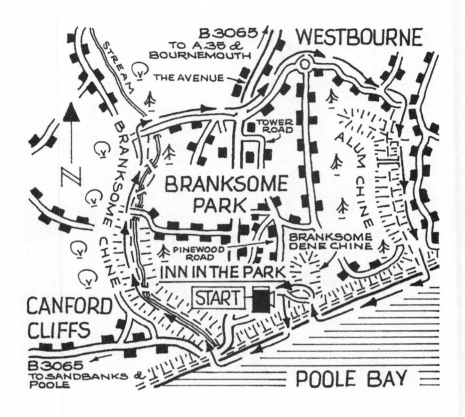

Stroll along the promenade, with lovely golden sands to your left, until you arrive at a car park and a white-rendered restaurant at the bottom end of Branksome Chine, the longest of the Bournemouth chines. Walk past the restaurant until you see a walled path to the right, just before reaching steps giving access to balconied chalets. Follow the path up to the road and cross by means of the pedestrian refuge to enter the chine, laid out in gardens back in 1930. A small walled-in stream occupies the valley floor and you keep this in sight, crossing it occasionally as you walk up the ravine, where pines, oaks and sweet chestnuts stand like sentinels above you and varied shrubs occupy the spaces below. There are ornamental rock gardens and a nicely constructed stone bridge on the way up to meet and cross Tower Road West. Continue on the path through woodland on the other side of the road to soon reach Western Road.

Turn right to follow the road uphill to cross The Avenue at the traffic lights and continue along Western Road as far as a roundabout. Cross directly over to join Alum Chine Road opposite. A little way along here, you will pass the Robert Louis Stevenson memorial gardens to the right. This is the site of Skerryvore, a house where he passed the final two years of his life, from April 1885 to August 1887. The house overlooked the deep, wooded chasm of Alum Chine to the rear. Go around a right-hand bend into West Cliff Road, and look out for a footpath sign on the right showing the way to Alum Chine and the beach. This is at the bottom of the hill before you reach the block of flats called Chine Lodge.

Join the metalled, winding path to a bridge over the ravine and continue along the chine, ignoring another bridge to the left. There is no stream in the chine these days and the valley bottom has been levelled out. Pass under a spectacular suspension bridge and follow the wide metalled path past the car park and back to the promenade. Turn right and enjoy the seascape on your left, while crumbling, water-eroded sandstone cliffs rise to your right. Signs warn of unstable cliffs as you pass over the Bournemouth–Poole dividing line.

By a conical-roofed ice-cream shop displaying tourist information panels, turn right and mount two flights of steps into Branksome Dene car park. As you enter, go left and toil up the 27 concrete steps to the upper car park. Cross directly over and climb further steps to a viewing point furnished with seats. Suitably rested, go left-handed along the path to join the access road back up to Pinewood Road. Turn left and return to the pub.

Places of interest nearby

The beautiful gardens of *Compton Acres* await your visit. The entrance is off Canford Cliffs Road and you will be fascinated by the Japanese Garden, the Water Garden, the Heather Dell and many other features (telephone: 01202 700778).

⑬ Longham
The Angel

This pub, with its cottage-like appearance, gives you an urge to stop and sample its hospitality. It has retained a charming rural aspect in harmony with the village of Longham, which is an oasis surrounded by large areas of modern development. The actual date and origin of the pub are not known, but it certainly existed in 1780. The bar area is large yet cosy, with a myriad of world banknotes festooning the beams. An extension on the left-hand side was opened in 1993 and blends in admirably with the older section.

This is a Badger inn and serves Badger Best, BXB, Tanglefoot and Worthington Dark. If you fancy a lager, you can choose from Hofbrau or Pilsner. The food on offer is varied and plentiful. There is a four-page menu which should suit all tastes, with dishes ranging from double jumbo sausages and egg to wholetail scampi and prime rump steak. Szechuan chicken and Chinese beef may also tempt you and there are additional items for the evening. There is also a specials board. Children have their own menu and are welcome in the dining area. Salads, sandwiches, toasties and filled French sticks are available, with vegetarians having a good choice. There is a large patio to the rear, with a children's play space beyond which includes five trampolines. A surveillance monitor in the bar helps parents keep a check on the play area. Dogs are not allowed in the pub.

The pub is open from 11 am to 2.30 pm and 5.30 pm to 11 pm on Monday to Saturday, and from 12 noon to 3 pm and 7 pm to 10.30 pm on Sunday. Food is served at lunchtime from 12 noon to 2 pm and in the evening from 6 pm (7 pm on Sunday) to 9.30 pm.

Telephone: 01202 873778.

How to get there: Longham lies on the A348 Poole to Ferndown road. The Angel will be found to the north of the junction with the B3073.

Parking: There is ample parking on the left-hand side of the pub.

Length of the walk: 3½ miles. OS maps: Pathfinder 1301 and Land-ranger 195 Bournemouth, Purbeck and surrounding area (inn GR 068991).

Meadow and woodland combine to give a pleasant flavour to this circuit, with the river Stour not far away. The small village of Hampreston, with its attractive stone church set in a truly pastoral landscape, is visited on the walk.

The Walk

Leave the inn and carefully cross the main road. Join the gravelled track opposite, named Angel Lane, to walk down to a junction by Greenacres. Turn left along a shady track. As this bends right, cross the stile adjacent to the gate labelled 'Coneygar Farm'. Where the track bears right into the farmyard, go straight ahead along a short, hedged path to a stile. Cross this and go through a facing gate into a meadow. Follow the left-hand hedge as it bends left and proceed to a footbridge, where you turn right at a junction of paths.

A pleasant, right-hand field edge path now takes you alongside woodland. Look for the tower of Hampreston church peeping out between trees away to your left. It is 14th century with 19th-century additions and was formerly a chapel of Wimborne Minster. Soon the path becomes a track and you join Stapehill Road by the side of Stapehill Lodge. Turn left and walk up to the crossroads, where you go over to enter the lane leading to Hampreston. Watch out for Granville Cottage and the school to your right. You will see an architectural similarity between the buildings, with the same coat of arms fashioned in stone above the windows. This shield is that of the Greathead family of Uddens House who once owned these lands.

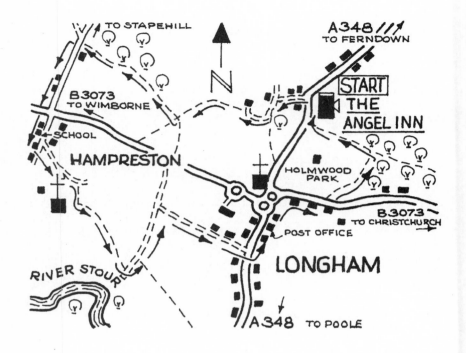

Take a track to the left, signed to the church and Longham Bridge. As you approach Hampreston church, veer left to pass on the left of a metal gate. The church, with its low tower, is of typically Dorset style and built in local stone. It is normally locked, but you can acquire a key from the house on the right. From the metal gate, proceed on a track to where a path soon turns right along a line of trees. Follow this to cross a stile and turn left, keeping a fence on your left. To the right you can see the former river bank quite prominently in the meadow. The Stour is now some 300 metres away, hidden in trees across the floodplain. As you approach a pylon, cross over a stile on your left and then turn right to follow a hedgeside path, descending to a sunken track and turning left.

Follow the track to a junction, where you go right to take up a track known as Green Lane, leading to Ringwood Road. Turn left to pass the post office and the White Hart Inn. The inn is 350 years old and was owned, in the late 18th century, by Isaac Gulliver, a well-known local smuggler. The turreted United Reformed church, which stands at the junction, was built in 1841. Bear right into Christchurch Road and walk past houses and bungalows. Shortly before the road bends left, look for a

Victorian cottages at Hampreston.

footpath sign on the left opposite a white bungalow (no 44). Cross the road and follow the path through a narrow defile to a stile. Cross this and go up the left-hand side of a meadow to another stile.

Cross the stile and enter woodland which has been invaded by rhododendrons growing densely beneath the oaks. Continue through this thicket up to a path crossing. Turn left and left again as the path emerges from the wood into a clear grassy area. Your path immediately re-enters the woodland and you bear left at two successive junctions. Both of these junctions are waymarked. Soon a meadow appears on the right. Veer right by gates and right again as you join a track to reach Ringwood Road. The Angel is close by on your right.

Places of interest nearby

If you follow the A348 southwards to the mini roundabouts and then go right into Ham Lane (the B3073), turning right again at the crossroads into Stapehill Road, you will see *Knoll Gardens* on your right. They are well worth a visit and now display over 4,000 different plant species. The gardens are open from 10 am to 6 pm every day from March to early November and contain ponds, waterfalls, a tearoom and a restaurant (telephone: 01202 873931).

⑭ Avon
The New Queen

If you fancy a little legend and romance, come to Avon – perhaps better known as Avon Tyrrell – where Sir Walter Tyrrell forded the river Avon in his flight from the assassination or otherwise of William Rufus, deep in the New Forest on 2nd August 1100. There was no pub in those days where Sir Walter could have gulped down a pint of ale in his haste, but there is now, in fact there has been one hereabouts for quite a few centuries. You may scratch your head and wonder why it is called the New Queen, and, with due respect to the sign painter, wonder who the new queen was. I did not recognise Elizabeth I, but I assure you that is who it is! Up to about 1700, the pub, then called the Queen, stood on the opposite side of the road, but after devastation by fire, it was rebuilt in its present position – hence 'the New Queen'.

This is a fine, low-ceilinged hostelry with plenty of atmosphere, carpeted throughout and with interesting different levels. There are round-backed wooden chairs and small, intimate tables. Fascinating alcoves and wooden balustrading complete the picture inside and a door leads off into a pleasant, spacious waterside garden.

A Hall & Woodhouse pub, Badger Best, BXB and Tanglefoot are on offer, with Ringwood Best as a guest ale. In addition, you will find Worthington Dark, a selection of lagers and Dry Blackthorn cider on tap. The food menu lists a good range of starters and main courses including 'Olde English' steak, plaice Dieppe, 'Surf and Turf' and rainbow trout. There are also home-made specialities such as Lancashire hot pot and macaroni and mushrooms as well as a selection for the smaller appetite and a specials board. Desserts include rhubarb crumble and hazelnut ice bonnet. There is a family area and a playground section for children in the garden. Well-behaved dogs are allowed in the bar.

The opening times are from 11 am to 3 pm and 6 pm to 11 pm on Monday to Saturday, and from 12 noon to 3 pm and 7 pm to 10.30 pm on Sunday. Food is served from 12 noon to 2.30 pm and 6.30 pm to 9 pm on Monday to Saturday, and from 12 noon to 2.30 pm and 7 pm to 9 pm on Sunday.

Telephone: 01425 672432.

How to get there: The hamlet of Avon lies on the B3347 Christchurch to Ringwood road, about 1½ miles north of Sopley.

Parking: There is ample parking to the side of the pub.

Length of the walk: 3½ miles. OS maps: Outdoor Leisure 22 New Forest, and Landranger 195 Bournemouth, Purbeck and surrounding area (inn GR 146896).

For those of you who do not like hills, this is an ideal walk, as there is not one slope on the route! This is cereal (mainly wheat and maize) and pig farming country and you may hear a few grunts as you go along. A pleasant, easy circuit, mainly on lanes and footpaths.

The Walk

Leave the pub and turn right along the main road. There are delightful views over the Avon valley to the right as you walk past the fine, thatched Avon Cottage on the same side. After passing a quaint brick farmhouse, also on the right, look for a stile and footpath sign on the left-hand side, adjacent to a pink-washed cottage. Cross the stile and proceed down the right-hand margin of a field, ignoring a gap to the right. Your route veers inwards to avoid three pine trees before you cross another stile to maintain your course down the right-hand edge of the next field. Continue over another stile before reaching a narrow strip of woodland, which you cross by two further stiles to meet the Avon Valley Path, which wends its way along the Avon valley between Christchurch and Salisbury.

Your acquaintance with this long-distance path is brief. Turn left onto it

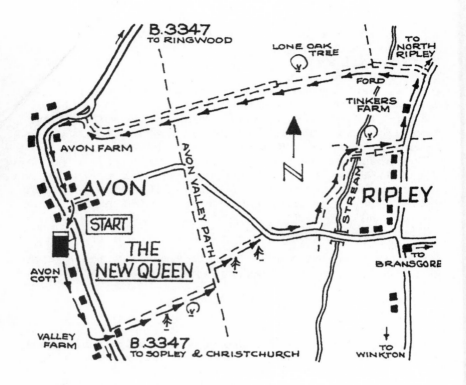

and pass over a stile, through another woodland strip and over yet another stile. Here you turn right alongside woodland, and leave the Avon Valley Path. Proceed down the right-hand field edge, with Hackthorn Plantation to your right. The path soon takes you over a stile to join a quiet country lane, which you follow to the right around a left-hand bend. As the lane soon swings right, you will see a two-armed footpath sign just before a bridge. Turn left here to pass through a gate or over the adjacent waymarked stile.

This is a particularly attractive part of the walk as you follow the path alongside another woodland strip, with a stream gliding through the trees as your companion on the right. Away, further to the right, are the cottages comprising the hamlet of Ripley. Salway's Plantation is the name of the wooded strip you are following. As you approach the field corner, your path goes sharply right to enter the woodland. Go right again over a single-railed footbridge over the stream you have been accompanying. Soon your path becomes a track and meets a lane, where you turn left.

Stile encountered on the walk.

Walk along this rural lane, past Tinkers Farm to where the lane swings left by a white-rendered house. On the left, you will see a track leading to two gates, one of which warns of 'Minimal Pig Disease' in the field beyond. Take the left of the two gates and follow the track to a ford, which you cross by means of a footbridge. Where the main track bends right to a gate, continue ahead on a lesser track to the edge of a vast arable field. Take the defined path ahead, aiming to the left of a half dead oak tree, to join a straight track over flat farmland. Near a chunky oak tree you cross over the Avon Valley Path. Follow the track as it bends right to meet the main road. Turn left and walk back to the pub, pausing to admire the Avon Farm house on the right.

Places of interest nearby

Just up the Ringwood road and signed to the right is the *New Forest Owl Sanctuary*, open to visitors between 10 am and 5 pm each day from 1st March to 5th November, and at weekends for the rest of the year. There are over 100 aviaries, an owl hospital, flying displays, lectures and videos for you to enjoy. Strangely enough, the Owl Sanctuary is at a place called Crow!

15 **Fairmile**
The Fairmile

As Christchurch pushed outwards between the rivers Stour and Avon, so Fairmile developed in modern times beneath the pine-clad heights of St Catherine's Hill. Fairmile Road stretches long and straight and the pub, built to serve the social needs of the area, presents an attractive and rather appealing façade to the passing traveller. A fine frontal extension was added to the building not so long ago and this houses a pleasant, carpeted restaurant-style area, with a part pine roof, and comfortable wall seating. There are two separate bars, and gardens to the front and rear.

This is a Whitbread house and you may also find Flowers Original and Boddingtons, but the real ales do change. Heineken or Stella Artois are the lagers, while Strongbow and Scrumpy Jack ciders are on draught. There is a good variety of food and it can be enjoyed anywhere in the pub – or outside. In addition to the wide choice on the standard menu, a specials board offers dishes like minty lamb casserole, cold meat platter and vegetable moussaka and chips. There are some interesting desserts to follow and a children's menu which includes Golden Tiddlers and Turkey Dinosaur. Children are allowed in the restaurant area and well-behaved dogs are permitted inside the pub.

The Fairmile is an 'all day' pub and is open from 11 am to 11 pm on Monday to Saturday, and from 12 noon to 10.30 pm on Sunday. Food can be ordered from 12 noon to 2 pm (2.30 pm in summer) and 7 pm to 9 pm every day.
Telephone: 01202 473499.

How to get there: Fairmile lies on the B3073 road between Christchurch and Hurn. The pub can be found just over a mile north of the junction with the western end of the A35 Christchurch bypass.

Parking: There is good parking at the rear of the pub, together with some space at the side.

Length of the walk: 3½ miles. OS maps: Outdoor Leisure 22 New Forest, and Landranger 195 Bournemouth, Purbeck and surrounding area (inn GR 147943).

Fine views, pine-clad hills and the typical heaths of south-east Dorset are strongly featured in this walk. The heathland, at times, seems incredibly wild and remote, bearing in mind how close it is to modern housing.

The Walk

As you leave the pub, turn left past the garage and shops to cross the busy Fairmile Road by the pelican crossing. Walk past another shopping parade to soon turn right onto a gravel track, which immediately forks. Take the left fork, called St Catherine's Hill Lane and signed as a bridleway to Avon Causeway. The track climbs gently past a white bungalow on the right to enter woodland of birch and oak. As you reach the gate leading to Christchurch Gun Club, veer right and pass by a gate signed 'No motor cycles'. The track now steepens and winds its way up the flank of St Catherine's Hill. Ignore all lesser side tracks and paths as you go up the hill. There are glimpses of extensive views to the right over the Avon valley and towards the New Forest. The track curves left and goes through a cluster of pines before levelling out.

There are many side paths hearabouts marked with the 'No Cycling' logo, but you ignore these and maintain your northerly course on the main track. After passing an open area of heathland on the left, the woodland becomes predominantly pine and you walk on a soft bed of pine needles. This is the summit of St Catherine's Hill and legend has it that a church was to be built up here but building materials were mysteriously moved overnight to the site where Christchurch Priory now stands. Pass a covered reservoir on the left and an information panel to the right overlooking an old sand and gravel extraction pit. Your track now gently

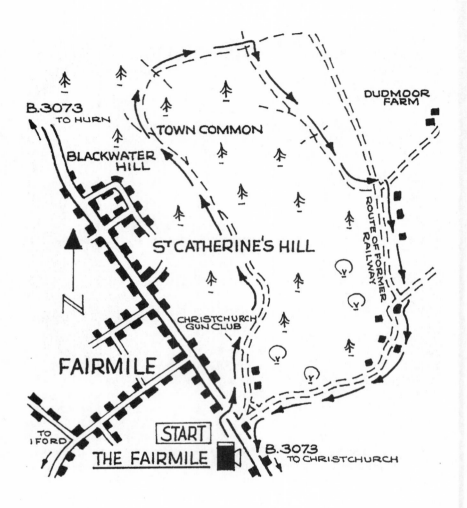

descends through pine woodland into a cleared valley and rises again fairly sharply. Blue bridleway signs on posts keep you on the correct route. There is a further shallow drop and rise in the track. Extensive views and the hum of traffic on the nearby A338 become more prominent as the ridge narrows considerably.

Once more you go sharply down, turning half-left at the bottom to go briefly uphill and then plunge down through a sandy gully framed by pines. The sand is quite deep as you descend steeply, going right where the path forks by a silver birch tree. Continue the descent through rhodo-

A sandy path through the pines, on the walk from Fairmile.

dendrons, picking your way through much erosion under electricity transmission lines. Go over a small path crossing as your path becomes stony.
Soon you arrive at a big crossing of paths, where you turn right past a
sign saying 'Permissive bridleway. Oct 20–April 20 only please'. This
restriction does not apply to walkers and you proceed as the path widens
and crosses a low hill under the same transmission lines as you encountered earlier. You descend again, with heath ponds to the left and the
flanks of the St Catherine's Hill ridge to the right. After veering right to
avoid a boggy area, you meet another path and go left.

Pass another 'permissive bridleway' sign and keep ahead at a path
crossing, still following the base of the ridge on your right. Walk past a

'No horses or bikes' sign and soon you share your path with a little stream. Over this section, the path narrows to a minimum through heather and moor grass, but you soon bend left to meet a gravel road opposite to the entrance to Dudmoor Farm. Turn right here to follow the route of the old Ringwood to Christchurch railway, built in 1862. Several properties have access to this well-used track, including Cresswell, which has a nature information panel at its entrance. Trees shade the route of the former railway, which is raised on a low embankment above wetlands. Soon you join Dudmoor Farm Road and turn right and then quickly left along a well-used gravel track. Ignore all side turnings as you follow the track back to Fairmile Road – a distance of about ½ mile. Turn left past the shops, back to the pub.

Places of interest nearby

The award-winning *Alice in Wonderland* beckons you and is only just to the north up the B3073, off Parley Lane opposite Hurn Airport (now Bournemouth International Airport). Here you can join Alice and her friends and tackle the unique maze. You will also find the Queen of Hearts' crazy croquet lawn, a human-sized rabbit warren, the Mad Hatter's Tea Gardens and the Cheshire Cat's Adventure Playground. Listen to story telling and visit the farmyard and gardens. Open from early April to the end of October (telephone: 01202 483444).

Southbourne
The Commodore Hotel

16

If you would like to enjoy a drink, sample well-cooked food and at the same time savour a glorious seascape over Poole Bay, framed by the Needles to the east and Durlston Head to the west, come along to the Commodore on Southbourne's Overcliff Drive and do just that! On a bracing day with cotton wool cumuli flecking a blue sky, there is no finer spot than this. The Commodore is actually a hotel with 15 rooms, but it has that unmistakable 'pubby' feel in the long bar downstairs. In common with most of Southbourne, it is relatively new, and way back in the 1950s it was a seafront café.

There are four real ales on offer, Wadworth 6X, Boddingtons, Pompey Royal and Flowers Original, in addition to Whitbread beers. Stella Artois and Heineken should satisfy lager lovers, and draught and bottled ciders are also served. The Commodore has a Berni menu, served up by friendly, attentive staff. Steaks are to the fore, ranging from a 5 oz rump steak to a massive 32 oz specimen. Fish dishes, vegetarian meals and a range of starters complement the steaks, grills, main dishes and salads, with a good selection of desserts to follow. If your appetite is small, there are sandwiches and Berni baps. A specials board lists other choices, and a roast is always available on a Sunday. There are a few tables outdoors for use on warm days. Children are allowed in the pub and there is a no smoking area to the left. Only guide dogs are permitted in the bar.

The pub rarely closes its doors and you will be welcome from 11 am to 11 pm on Monday to Saturday, and from 12 noon to 10.30 pm on Sunday. Food is available from 12 noon to 9 pm every day.

Telephone: 01202 423150 or 427127.

How to get there: Southbourne lies between the Bournemouth to Christchurch road (the A35) and the sea. Take the B3059 (Parkwood Road) just east of Boscombe town centre. Turn second right along Beechwood Avenue and continue ahead at the crossroads to go down Woodlands Avenue to reach Overcliff Drive where you turn left. The Commodore is about ½ mile along on the left.

Parking: The pub has a small parking area at the front and you can park in surrounding roads.

Length of the walk: 3 miles. OS maps: Outdoor Leisure 22 New Forest, and Landranger 195 Bournemouth, Purbeck and surrounding area (inn GR 130913).

This relaxing and easy walk gives splendid views over Poole Bay, to Hengistbury Head, the Isle of Wight and the Needles, and Durlston Head backed by the Purbeck Hills. A walk along the clifftop is followed by a gentle return stroll along the Undercliff promenade – a complete contrast to the busy promenades and beaches of Bournemouth and Boscombe.

The Walk

Leave the pub to cross Overcliff Drive by way of the handy pelican crossing and head seawards on the path leading to Fisherman's Walk lift. Only go as far as the first metalled path on the left to ensure that you remain on the clifftop to enjoy the wonderful seaward views. Seats and a shelter line your route as the path wends its way over manicured clifftop grassland. Several seats are dedicated to lost loved ones, as many couples retire here to enjoy the favoured climate of the South Coast. The path moves closer to the clifftop and begins to undulate more. Look down and see fine golden sands below but don't be tempted to stray down as you will return that way. As your immediate surroundings become a little wilder, look back and savour the distant line of the Purbeck Hills and the tall flats, offices and hotels of Bournemouth.

As you rejoin Southbourne Overcliff Drive, turn right. Houses and bungalows briefly interrupt your seascape views, but this is only temporary.

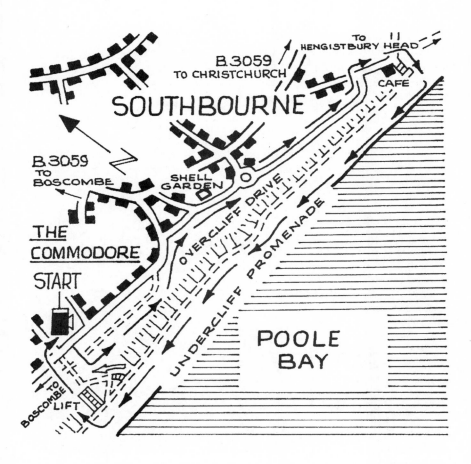

Soon the Isle of Wight's cliffs return into sight, and if you are lucky enough to have a clear day, you may be able to pick out St Catherine's Point, the most southerly tip of the island. A novelty now presents itself on the opposite side of the road. You must cross over and see 'the world's most unique shell garden'. This must have taken years to construct and the end product of myriad shells, tiles and mosaics fashioned into gardens, fountains and waterfalls is well worth the admiring comments and clicking cameras it attracts.

Soon you arrive at a roundabout, not far away from the shops of Southbourne. Keep right here and maintain your route near the cliff edge. This is the Southbourne Coast Road and leads downhill past the Warren Edge car park. Proceed eastwards past a pleasantly green clifftop area on

Expansive views on the approach to Hengistbury Head.

the right, furnished with seats. As you reach a junction, turn right past the Point House Café where you can call in for tea, coffee and light refreshments. Just after the café, steps descend to the lower promenade on the right. Before this, pause and look over to Hengistbury Head. The summit, marked by the coastguard station, is a little under 1½ miles away and a gravelled path leads directly there (but a detour would, of course, add nearly 3 miles to your walk). This quite famous headland is an ancient monument and has a history dating back to the Stone Age. Double dykes protect the landward side and were built by the Celts 2,000 years ago.

Go down the steps to the lower promenade, which you actually join at its eastern terminal (the western terminal is at Sandbanks). Turn right and stroll along the base of a low cliff. This is a sheltered promenade and at most times of the year on sunny days you will see people sitting out and enjoying the view. Frequent groynes protect the excellent sandy beach from unwanted erosion. As you walk along, the cliffs of sandstone and gravel become higher, and at one point you will see a house teetering on the edge. The cliffs hereabouts are quite lofty and show signs of water erosion in places, with wire framed gabions built in to support the soft sandstone. They heighten even further as the path veers seaward to pass around a sandy bluff, and soon 'Gordons Zig Zag' coils away up the cliff to Overcliff Drive.

As you arrive at a substantial stone-faced retaining wall, you can either walk up the steps or ramp to return to the clifftop, or take the Fisherman's Walk lift which is a few steps further on. The lift operates 9.30 am to 5.30 pm daily and until 6.15 pm during the school holidays. Charges are 40p for adults and 20p for children. Once on the top, the Commodore Hotel is directly in view ahead.

Places of interest nearby

If you head towards Bournemouth along Overcliff Drive, turn right up Chessel Avenue past Shelley Park, and then turn left into Beechwood Avenue, you will find the *Shelley Museum* interesting to browse around. There is a ½ hour's video of the poet's life to see. The museum is open on Tuesday to Saturday from 2 pm to 5 pm and is free (telephone: 01202 303571). There is also the *Russell Cotes Art Gallery and Museum* in Russell Cotes Road, East Cliff, Bournemouth, which is open on Tuesday to Sunday from 10 am to 5 pm and is also free of charge (telephone: 01202 551009 or 551500).

⑰ Sopley
The Woolpack

Take a quaint English village with an old church on a hill, overlooking a river. Take pretty cottages and a stream gliding through trees and under a little bridge by a fine, thatched village inn – and you have Sopley, quieter and more serene now that the former A338 traffic has gone away.

The beer mats in the Woolpack say 'Your 17th-century musical pub' – not Beethoven or Delius, but talented pianists playing soft music as you eat and drink. You can hear the pianist on Thursday, Friday and Saturday evening and at lunchtime on Thursday and Sunday. This popular inn is a Whitbread house, offering real ales such as Ringwood Best, Wadworth 6X and Flowers Original. There are various lagers and Murphy's Irish Stout on tap. You can drink in the bars, out on the splendid terrace or in the attractive conservatory restaurant. The food is good and varied, with seafood figuring prominently. There is an extensive bar menu and extra choices in the evening. A range of seven starters is followed by a wide main course selection, including Old Thumper sausages, avocado bake topped with peppers and cheese sauce, cod in beer batter and the Woolpack's famous smoked seafood pie – or you may prefer fresh mussels poached in white wine, cream, garlic and coriander. There are many desserts to choose from, such as 'Toffee Crunch Cheesequake', sachertorte served with cream, or assorted ice-creams and sorbets. Well-behaved children are allowed in the pub, and dogs are welcome in the bar. There is a pleasant, shaded garden over a footbridge if you want to sit outdoors. With all this and music too, you cannot go wrong! Greta Garbo once had a drink here while she was staying with an artist friend in Ringwood.

The Woolpack is open from 11 am to 11 pm on Monday to Saturday, and from 12 noon to 3 pm and 7 pm to 10.30 pm on Sunday. Food is available from 12 noon to 2 pm and 6.30 pm to 9.30 pm every day.

Telephone: 01425 672252.

How to get there: Sopley lies on the B3347 Christchurch to Ringwood road. The Woolpack can be found at the southern end of the village one-way system.

Parking: The pub has a car park. You can also park on the road.

Length of the walk: 3 miles. OS maps: Outdoor Leisure 22 New Forest, and Landranger 195 Bournemouth, Purbeck and surrounding area (inn GR 156968).

This route takes you along some of the pleasant little lanes and interesting field paths that are a feature of the lower Avon valley. During the walk, you will pass along two sections of the three counties Avon Valley Path, distinctive with its bridge logo. It wends its way for 34 miles from Christchurch to Salisbury.

The Walk

Emerge from the pub and join the northbound section of Sopley's one-way system. Turn left to pass over the bridge at the front of the inn. Go directly over the road to the entrance to Moorlands College, a Christian Training Centre guarded by a turreted brick lodge. You will see a footpath sign announcing the Avon Valley Path as you enter the driveway. Shortly along this, you will see a metal kissing-gate to the left with Avon Valley Path markers. Pass through this and go right, soon curving away from the driveway to meet a stile which you cross. Turn right to follow the field edge as it gradually swings left. Cross another stile, with a house showing to your right, and soon enter a narrow paddock by way of a stile on the right. Obliquely left, you will see a further stile which you cross to follow the same alignment over a large meadow, passing to the right of a cattle trough and to the left of a mid-field beech tree. Crossing two more stiles with a woodland strip in between brings you out onto a narrow lane, where you part company with the Avon Valley Path.

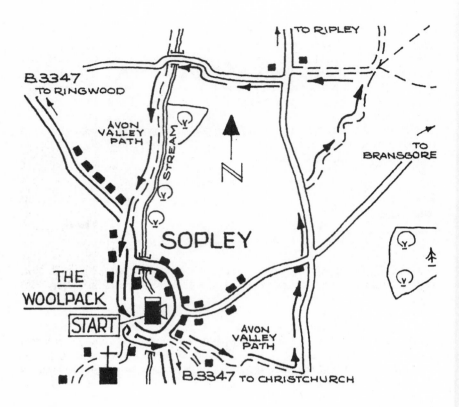

Turn left and follow this pleasant, hedged lane to go over the Sopley to Bransgore road and continue up the lane opposite, signed to Ripley. After about 350 yards, look for a footpath sign on the right at the end of a green-meshed, concrete-posted fence. Join the footpath, keeping the fence to your left and enjoying the gloriously open countryside before you, with the dark trees of the New Forest on the horizon. Keep the fence to your immediate left and follow all its bends and kinks. Eventually it becomes a broken hedge with firstly ash and then oaks lining your route and you reach a stile. Cross this to meet a track. Ignore inviting footpath signs to your right and turn left to follow the track until you meet a lane.

As you meet the lane, turn left and then immediately right to join another. Stroll along this pleasant lane to pass around an 'S' bend and walk over a little brick bridge. The stream trickling happily underneath is the same one which flows through the garden of the Woolpack pub, and it will escort you back there. Just beyond the bridge, turn left to pass

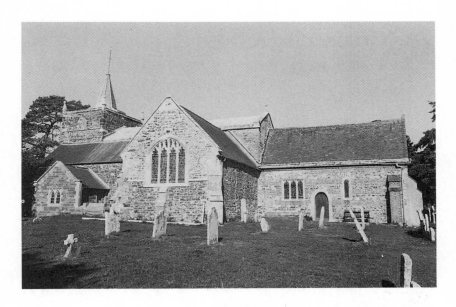

Sopley church.

through a wooden kissing-gate and rejoin your old friend, the Avon Valley Path. Three stiles in succession (one appearing to be moribund) take you to the left-hand edge of a large arable field. Continue down the side of this, with the stream not far away, hidden in the trees to your left. Eventually you reach and cross a stile.

To me, the most attractive part of the walk now greets you, as the path becomes a wide strip of grass bounded by trees and an ample hedge. Soon it changes character still further, becoming shadily overhung with young oaks, hazel and ash, with the stream visible in the trees to your left. Before long, the backs of houses appear on the right, and reluctantly you leave this delightful section of path to cross a stile and emerge onto the B3347. Cross over the road and walk down past the village stores and post office. Keep to the right at the start of the village one-way system and make your way back to the inn, taking care as there is no pavement.

Places of interest nearby

Stewart's Garden Lands, just outside Christchurch on the A35 Lyndhurst road, is very well worth a visit. Stroll around the amazing display of houseplants, herbaceous plants, shrubs and ornamental trees. There are gardening talks held in the greenhouse, and a coffee shop where you can have a drink and a snack (telephone: 01425 278820).

Christchurch
The Kings Arms Hotel – Kings Bar

18

The Kings Bar, joined by swing doors to the main hotel, offers a truly ancient scene as you take a window seat to sample your food and drink. The view takes in the ruins of the Constable's House, the Keep and the venerable Priory itself, a good range of Norman and Early English architecture. This is an old-fashioned town bar, with traditional décor and with its full share of local folk chatting over a pint. There has been a pub here since 1670, called the Kings Arms Inn in those days. It was pulled down to be replaced by a hotel in 1801, known as 'Humby's' after Thomas Humby, its first landlord, and changed to its present name following his death in 1820.

The Kings Bar offers a simple menu with starters, fish dishes and chef's specials, including old favourites like steak pie and chicken curry. Vegetarians are not forgotten and can enjoy courgette and Brie crumble or nut paella. There is also a good range of 'Kings' sandwiches. When food is not available in the Kings Bar, you can cross over to the Toby Grill in the hotel and order food from a more extensive menu. Lunchtime specials are offered here, with children having their own menu of starter, main course and dessert. In the friendly Kings Bar, you can drink Bass,

Worthington Best and Caffrey's Irish Ale, or Carling Premier and Black Label if you fancy a lager. Guinness and Dry Blackthorn cider are available on tap. Dogs are not welcome inside the pub. There is a very small garden, but it is interesting to wander over Castle Street to the municipal gardens by the Constable's House to see 'Kings Arms Hotel tea gardens' inscribed in the concrete of the access gateway. An echo of yesteryear!

Opening times at both the Kings Bar and the Toby Grill are from 11 am to 3 pm and 6 pm to 11 pm on Monday to Thursday, 11 am to 11 pm on Friday and Saturday, and 12 noon to 3 pm and 7 pm to 10.30 pm on Sunday. Food is available in the Kings Bar from 12 noon to 2 pm and 6 pm to 8 pm on Monday to Thursday. Saturday hours are from 12 noon to 2 pm, but there is no food in the evening or at any time on Friday or Sunday. The Toby Grill offers food from 12 noon to 10 pm on Sunday, with ordering times during the rest of the week being 12 noon to 2.30 pm and 6 pm to 10.30 pm (11 pm on Friday and Saturday).

Telephone: 01202 484117.

How to get there: From the Bournemouth/Poole direction, the town would be best approached by way of the A35 from Iford Bridge. At the kidney-shaped roundabout at the western end of the Christchurch bypass (A35), turn right down the High Street (B3073) to the town centre and then follow the B3073 left into Castle Street. The Kings Arms Hotel is on the left.

Parking: Parking is available to the side of the hotel. There are also public car parks in Bridge Street and at the Leisure Centre nearby.

Length of the walk: 3 miles. OS maps: Outdoor Leisure 22 New Forest, and Landranger 195 Bournemouth, Purbeck and surrounding area (inn GR 159927).

Christchurch is a fascinating town lying on the twin estuaries of the Avon and the Stour. This walk takes you around the interesting Stanpit Marshes, alive with all types of birds, especially at migratory times. There are cormorants, grebes, coots, egrets and many others. If you are lucky, you may see the flashing blue of a kingfisher. As well as birdlife, enjoy lovely views over the river and marsh to Mudeford Spit, Hengistbury Head and the timeless Priory Church of Christchurch, whose bells often peel softly over the marshlands.

The Walk

Turn left from the Kings Arms Hotel and walk over the two Avon bridges, firstly the main channel of the Avon and then the lesser channel called the

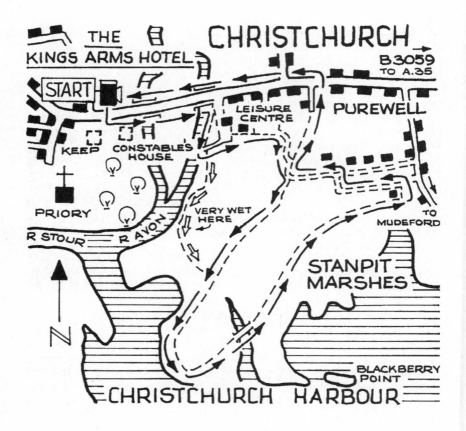

Little Avon. After the second bridge, cross over Bridge Street by the pelican crossing. Follow the pavement right-handed to pass over the zebra crossing and join a metalled path adjacent to a wall by the public toilets. Go over the steps to the right of the Civic Offices and take a waterside path as far as the entrance to Little Avon Marina.

There is an alternative route from here onwards that offers fine views over the marshlands if you are prepared for wet ground. Stay on the path by the marina and continue down to an information board, where you will see a stile to the right. Cross over to join the Little Avon river bank. As the waterway bends right, veer left and cross two short boardwalks, heading for a stile directly ahead. This section is very damp underfoot but leads you via stiles and footbridges to join the described walk route as shown on the map.

Little Avon Marina.

If you opt for a much drier route, turn left at the entrance to the Little Avon Marina and go past the end of the Civic Offices car park, taking the brick-paved pathway past the Riversmeet Leisure Centre and then keeping to the right-hand margin of the Leisure Centre car park. Leave the car park at the far end by passing to the left of a metal gate, and join a gravelled track.

Follow the track around several bends until you cross a water channel, where a path crosses the track. Turn right here and right again as the path quickly forks. With the Leisure Centre golf course up to your right, follow the waterside path to a kissing-gate. Pass through and go ahead, slightly right-handed, on a worn path through brambles. A fine view soon opens up with marshlands, waterways and the low bulk of Hengistbury Head in sight. It is an ill wind that does no one any good, because the world slump of 1929 prevented a Gothic folly castle being built on Hengistbury's summit. The next year, Bournemouth Corporation bought the headland to preserve as an open space. Your path, raised on a low causeway, stretches straight ahead over many footbridges. Glance over to the right to see the Priory tower showing above trees and boat masts. The alternative wet route joins from the right on this section.

The path takes you to the water's edge and you may feel a tinge of regret as you soon leave the estuary and cut across a peninsula to cross a metal-framed bridge over a water inlet, interestingly named Mother Sillers Channel. Follow the path ahead through scattered gorse bushes and past an information panel giving yesterday's bird sightings and general news. Go ahead, with a hedge on your left, and pass through a wooden kissing-gate. Continue to the left of a vehicle gate and past the Sea Scouts' hut. Turn left through the car park and left again to pass a gate and join a pathway surfaced in green felt-type material.

Your green-carpeted walkway changes to an ordinary surface as you bend right past a building and head towards new housing. Go left at the junction and pass over the bridge you crossed on the outward route. Retrace your steps for a short distance along the track and look out for a footbridge on the right as the track bends left. Cross this to walk along a confined, leafy path past dilapidated sheds, eventually passing over an estate road. The path soon joins the end of Marsh Lane, which you follow to the main road. Turn left and walk back to the Kings Arms Hotel.

Places of interest nearby

Christchurch is well worth exploring. Visit the *Priory*, where people have worshipped for a thousand years, and the *Keep* which has survived demolition attempts, together with the *Constable's House* nearby. Look around the waterside gardens and also the *Red House Museum* and gardens in Church Lane. Nearly opposite the Kings Arms is the *New Forest Perfumery*, where you can see and smell traditional perfumes. There is also a *tricycle museum* in Princess Quay.

Bransgore
The Three Tuns

Many years ago, there was a sound of chains clanking on the first floor of the Three Tuns, holding fast unhappy prisoners condemned at Winchester to exile for life. The pub was a staging post in their transit to the coast and then to the far away Antipodes. Prisoners certainly do not need to be taken now, as people flock here willingly to enjoy the food and drink – and then walk away free and contented. This is a fine, 16th-century, thatched, colourful inn with eleven acres of grounds, the extent of which harks back to mid century when it was a pig farm as well as a pub. A pleasant little restaurant beckons you from behind a wrought iron grille.

You can eat anywhere in the pub and be served by the efficient staff. There is a bar snack list and a main meal menu displayed on a board. Popular dishes are venison marinated in juniper berries and red wine, and breast of Barbary duck served with a wide range of sauces. Poached fillet of sea bass or grilled salmon may also tempt you. In addition, there is a good range of ploughman's lunches, sandwiches and desserts. The selection of drinks matches the wide variety of food. As well as Whitbread beers, you can sample Ringwood Fortyniner, Gale's HSB, Flowers Original and Boddingtons ales. For those who prefer a lager, Heineken and Stella

Artois are on offer, and if you fancy a cider, try the draught Scrumpy Jack. Whatever your taste in wine it should be met by the comprehensive wine list. Children are not specially catered for, but they are welcome in the snuggery or restaurant areas. There is also a spacious garden at the rear.

The inn awaits your custom from 11 am to 3 pm and 6 pm to 11 pm on Monday to Saturday, and from 12 noon to 3 pm and 7 pm to 10.30 pm on Sunday. Food is available every day from 12 noon to 2 pm and 6.30 pm (7 pm on Sunday) to 9 pm.

Telephone: 01425 672232.

How to get there: Bransgore can be reached from the A35 east of the Christchurch bypass. Turn off by the Cat and Fiddle pub at Hinton and follow signs to the village. After a little under 2 miles, you will find the Three Tuns on your left, just past the brick church.

Parking: There is plenty of parking to the side of the pub.

Length of the walk: 3½ miles. OS maps: Outdoor Leisure 22 New Forest, and Landranger 195 Bournemouth, Purbeck and surrounding area (inn GR 190975).

This walk takes you over fine pastoral land adjacent to the south-western fringes of the New Forest. Field paths and country lanes lead you through the gentlest of rural landscapes.

The Walk

Cross the road in front of the inn and turn right to pass the 100 year old village school and the Victorian brick church of St Mary the Virgin. Keep on the footway to cross the river Mude by a concrete footbridge and soon go left then right over a staggered crossroads. Proceed around an 'S' bend and over another crossroads at the hamlet of Godwinscroft. Continue along the road on the wide right-hand verge, past the entrance to New Close Farm. After a slight right-hand bend, take the gravelled track on the right, signed as a bridleway, and pass through the small metal gate to the left of a larger one.

The track now leads attractively towards distant pine woodland and as you reach this, the gravelled surface is left behind. A more extensive area of pines begins to show up ahead and there is a particularly fine row of mature trees on the right as you enter this, guarding the track like dark sentinels. Pass through another small metal gate adjacent to a larger double one to meet a further track. Turn right to join a narrow metalled lane which bends to the left by a house called Mellow Ridge. Go down past cottages on the right to a road junction, where you turn right.

You have now reached the pleasant little hamlet of Waterditch, a nice mix of old and new. Soon you are confronted by a 'Ford' sign, which always offers a delightful prospect of adventure ahead. The anticipation does not let you down as it is one of the prettiest little fords I have encountered, with a glinting brook gliding over the tree-shaded lane by Brook Cottage. Walk across the footbridge to the right, or wade – I recommend the latter if you have wellies on. Continue on up the leafy lane to reach eventually a triangular junction. Turn left and follow this lane to cross the river Mude again at a railed bridge. Shortly after this, you turn right by a prominent metal footpath sign.

You may hear the whistle of trains on the distant Bournemouth line as you go up a fenced, green trackway which ends as you enter a field. Keep the hedge on your right as you walk up the right-hand side of the field on a fairly well-defined path. As you bend right, pass through a waymarked gap at the field corner to walk along a low bank on the right-hand side margin of the next field. A gap in the hedge reveals the rippling river Mude, which you cross by way of a disappointing concrete slab footbridge when your path bends sharply right. Follow the well-defined path up along the left-hand side of a meadow, turning left to pass a ruined building. Shortly join a farm access track, where you turn right to soon join a lane.

Turn to the right and then almost immediately go left into the gravelled Chisels Lane. Houses in this area form part of the hamlet of Neacroft, which lies mainly to the north. Where the track forks, go left past a house called Chisels, the name displayed in mosaic tiles above the double garage. Cross the fence ahead by way of a gap or over a low, waymarked stile and go directly ahead into a large arable field along a defined path, well to the right of an electricity post. This brings you to a mid-field waymark post, where the path changes direction and goes obliquely left to a visible stile in the far hedgerow. Cross this to meet a lane and turn right. At a junction, go left and walk back to the pub.

Places of interest nearby

As you are so near to the New Forest, why not visit the typical Forest village of *Burley*, 4 miles away, with its pretty shops. You can take various horse-drawn wagon rides each day from 11 am to see the village and surrounding countryside. For further details, telephone: Burley Wagonettes (01425 672576).

20 Walkford
The Amberwood

What a delight it is to find a fine, traditional pub in an area of modern development. This is the true essence of England – discovering the unexpected in unlikely places. The cream-washed, red-shuttered pub, with its many gables and hanging baskets, will fascinate you. Step back and have a look at the frontage, and if you feel that it may have served other purposes, you are right. It began life as a coach house and stables to Amberwood House but by the 1940s had changed its character to that of a luxury residence, before becoming a country club ten years later. It was granted a licence in 1967 and became what it is now – a pub.

As you step inside, savour the spaciousness which greets you. Small circular tables, wheel-backed chairs and latticed windows give a good, old-fashioned feel to the premises. This is a Hall & Woodhouse pub selling Badger Best, Tanglefoot, Wadworth 6X and Charles Wells Eagle. There is also Hofbrau lager, alongside Dry Blackthorn cider. The food menu, supported by blackboard specials, offers a wide choice and you can eat in the bar or in the pleasant restaurant on the left. A main course selection to satisfy all tastes includes steak and kidney pie, chicken curry with rice and marinated knuckle of lamb with Greek salad. There are also grills and a good range of ordinary salads. Well-behaved dogs are welcome in the bar area and outside there are tables fringing the car park and a secluded walled garden, with a trampoline for children and seating.

You can enjoy a drink here all day, from 11 am to 11 pm on Monday to Saturday and from 12 noon to 10.30 pm on Sunday. Food is available from 12 noon to 2.30 pm each lunchtime and from 7 pm to 9.30 pm on Monday to Saturday evenings.

Telephone: 01425 272627.

How to get there: Walkford is best approached from the A35 Christchurch to Lyndhurst road, turning off by the Cat and Fiddle at Hinton. The pub is ½ mile along on the right.

Parking: The pub has an ample car park.

Length of the walk: 3½ miles. OS maps: Outdoor Leisure 22 New Forest, and Landranger 195 Bournemouth, Purbeck and surrounding area (inn GR 212947).

Although this walk is in an area of widespread residential development, pleasant woodland paths lead to the deep ravine known as Chewton Glen (or Chewton Bunny). A fine clifftop stroll follows, with sweeping views from the Needles around to Hengistbury Head and the Isle of Purbeck. The return route takes you back to the Amberwood by way of the surprisingly wild Chewton Common.

The Walk

Leave the pub, turning right to walk down Ringwood Road, past the Walkford shops and as far as Walkford Road. Turn left and continue until just before you reach the Walkford Inn, at which point you take the unmade Seaview Road on your right. Where this bends left, go straight ahead along a metalled footpath through oak and birch woodland. Cross Ringwood Road to continue on the path until you reach Lymington Road (the A337). Go across, with care, and follow the main road, left-handed, to the roundabout and continue down into the wooded Chewton Glen. Just before the bridge which spans the depths, turn right onto a signed footpath and then right again to follow the main path along the sylvan ravine. The Walkford Brook gurgles happily down on your left.

As you walk along, imagine the old-time smugglers heaving their contraband up the valley, probably as far as the Cat and Fiddle at Hinton. This pub was notorious back in smuggling days, being used as a distribution point for illicit goods. When you reach an access road by a signpost, turn left and then proceed straight ahead along a pea shingle driveway past

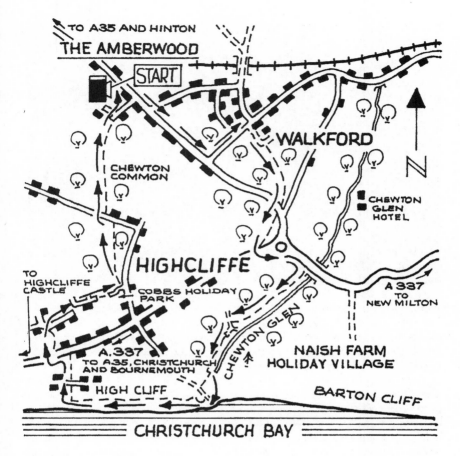

Tanglewood and Squirrel's Leap. The driveway soon reverts to a path, which you follow through continuing woodland until you see steps descending to the valley bottom on the left. Go down these and turn right at the lower end. The Walkford Brook disappears into a concrete culvert as you join a track leading to a metalled road. Turn left to pass steps on the right before turning right up a track towards an information pillar. Read all about the problems of Barton Cliffs before proceeding right-handed up the track to pass through bollards on to a concrete road.

Here you turn left to mount steps to a clifftop shelter. Pause to admire the broad sweep of Christchurch Bay and then walk on along the clifftop past the car park on the right. Eventually your path turns right by a sign reading 'Public Footpath to Lymington Road'. After enjoying open vistas,

A neat suburban bungalow, seen on the route.

you are suddenly confined between fences. Cross over Wharncliffe Road and pass along the right-hand side of a recreation ground to reach Lymington Road. Go over this busy highway by way of the pelican crossing and turn left. Look out for a metalled path on the right just after passing the entrance to Highcliffe Medical Centre. This short path leads down through woodland into Jesmond Avenue, where you go right.

Admire the neat bungalows and well-tended front gardens as you walk to the end of the cul-de-sac. Here you veer left into Merley Drive and follow this, right-handed, past Haslemere Avenue to the end of the road, where you will find a well-used path leading into woodland. This shaded path soon enters the Cobbs Holiday Park caravan site. Go round to the right of the first caravan and walk down the road to leave the park by swinging left at the junction (the site shop is immediately on your right). The access road curves right to soon meet Gordon Road. Turn left and then left again to join a nicely-shaded metalled path leading up to Chewton Common Road. Cross over, then turn left and soon right to join a signed pathway.

Ignoring all side paths, cross Chewton Common through heather, gorse and finally woodland to reach Pinewood Close. Walk directly up the road to meet Ringwood Road, where you turn left and return to the Amberwood.

Places of interest nearby

Highcliffe Castle is just over 1 mile to the south-west of Walkford. The grounds were opened to the public in June 1977 to celebrate the Queen's Silver Jubilee. The Kaiser stayed here for three weeks in 1907, and in 1916 Gordon Selfridge purchased the house to escape the menacing Zeppelins. The house suffered severe damage by fire in 1967. Eastwards along Walkford Road and Gore Road is *Sammy Miller's Motor Cycle Museum* which is open from 10 am to 4.30 pm each day. Telephone 01425 619696 for further information on this museum.